Lecture Notes in Computer Science 16157

Founding Editors

Gerhard Goos
Juris Hartmanis

Editorial Board Members

Elisa Bertino, *Purdue University, West Lafayette, IN, USA*
Wen Gao, *Peking University, Beijing, China*
Bernhard Steffen , *TU Dortmund University, Dortmund, Germany*
Moti Yung , *Columbia University, New York, NY, USA*

The series Lecture Notes in Computer Science (LNCS), including its subseries Lecture Notes in Artificial Intelligence (LNAI) and Lecture Notes in Bioinformatics (LNBI), has established itself as a medium for the publication of new developments in computer science and information technology research, teaching, and education.

LNCS enjoys close cooperation with the computer science R & D community, the series counts many renowned academics among its volume editors and paper authors, and collaborates with prestigious societies. Its mission is to serve this international community by providing an invaluable service, mainly focused on the publication of conference and workshop proceedings and postproceedings. LNCS commenced publication in 1973.

Bedir Tekinerdogan ·
Hassan Abdulsalam Hamid · Haifeng Li ·
Liang-Jie Zhang
Editors

Internet of Things – ICIOT 2025

10th International Conference
Held as Part of the Services Conference Federation, SCF 2025
Hong Kong, China, September 27–30, 2025, Proceedings

Editors
Bedir Tekinerdogan
Wageningen University
Wageningen, The Netherlands

Haifeng Li
Fuyang Normal University
Fuyang, China

Hassan Abdulsalam Hamid
Northern Technical University
Mosul, Iraq

Liang-Jie Zhang
Shenzhen University
Shenzhen, China

ISSN 0302-9743 ISSN 1611-3349 (electronic)
Lecture Notes in Computer Science
ISBN 978-3-032-06169-0 ISBN 978-3-032-06170-6 (eBook)
https://doi.org/10.1007/978-3-032-06170-6

© The Editor(s) (if applicable) and The Author(s), under exclusive license to Springer Nature Switzerland AG 2026

This work is subject to copyright. All rights are solely and exclusively licensed by the Publisher, whether the whole or part of the material is concerned, specifically the rights of translation, reprinting, reuse of illustrations, recitation, broadcasting, reproduction on microfilms or in any other physical way, and transmission or information storage and retrieval, electronic adaptation, computer software, or by similar or dissimilar methodology now known or hereafter developed.
The use of general descriptive names, registered names, trademarks, service marks, etc. in this publication does not imply, even in the absence of a specific statement, that such names are exempt from the relevant protective laws and regulations and therefore free for general use.
The publisher, the authors and the editors are safe to assume that the advice and information in this book are believed to be true and accurate at the date of publication. Neither the publisher nor the authors or the editors give a warranty, expressed or implied, with respect to the material contained herein or for any errors or omissions that may have been made. The publisher remains neutral with regard to jurisdictional claims in published maps and institutional affiliations.

This Springer imprint is published by the registered company Springer Nature Switzerland AG
The registered company address is: Gewerbestrasse 11, 6330 Cham, Switzerland

If disposing of this product, please recycle the paper.

Preface

With the rapid advancements of mobile Internet, cloud computing, and big data, the device-centric traditional Internet of Things (IoT) is now moving into a new era which is termed Internet of Things Services (IOTS). In this era, sensors and other types of sensing devices, wired and wireless networks, platforms and tools, data processing/visualization/analysis and integration engines, and other components of traditional IoT are interconnected through innovative services to realize the value of connected things, people, and virtual Internet spaces. The way of building new IoT applications is changing. We indeed need creative thinking, long-term visions, and innovative methodologies to respond to such a change. The ICIOT 2025 conference was organized to continue to promote research and application innovations around the world.

ICIOT 2025 was a member of the Services Conference Federation (SCF). SCF 2025 had the following 10 collocated service-oriented sister conferences: 2025 International Conference on Web Services (ICWS 2025), 2025 International Conference on Cloud Computing (CLOUD 2025), 2025 International Conference on Services Computing (SCC 2025), 2025 International Conference on Big Data (BigData 2025), 2025 International Conference on AI & Multimodal Services (AIMS 2025), 2025 International Conference on Metaverse (METAVERSE 2025), 2025 International Conference on Internet of Things (ICIOT 2025), 2025 International Conference on Cognitive Computing (ICCC 2025), 2025 International Conference on Edge Computing (EDGE 2025), and 2025 International Conference on Blockchain (ICBC 2025).

This volume presents the accepted papers of the 2025 International Conference on Internet of Things (ICIOT 2025), held in Hong Kong, China during September 27–30, 2025. For this conference, each paper was single-blind reviewed by three independent members of the International Program Committee. After carefully evaluating their originality and quality, we accepted 8 papers from 11 submissions.

We are pleased to thank the authors whose submissions and participation made this conference possible. We also want to express our thanks to the Organizing Committee and Program Committee members, for their dedication in helping to organize the conference and reviewing the submissions. We owe special thanks to the keynote speakers for their impressive speeches.

Finally, we would like to thank operations team members Jing Zeng, Sheng He, Yishuang Ning, and Zhuolin Mei for their excellent work in organizing this conference. We look forward to your future great contributions as a volunteer, author, and conference participant in the fast-growing worldwide services innovations community.

August 2025

Bedir Tekinerdogan
Hassan Abdulsalam Hamid
Haifeng Li
Liang-Jie Zhang

Organization

Program Chairs

Bedir Tekinerdogan — Wageningen University, Netherlands
Hassan Abdulsalam Hamid — Northern Technical University, Iraq
Haifeng Li — Fuyang Normal University, China

Services Conference Federation (SCF 2025)

General Chairs

Ali Arsanjani — Google, USA
Wu Chou — Essenlix Corporation, USA

Coordinating Program Chair

Liang-Jie Zhang — Shenzhen University, China

CFO and International Affairs Chair

Min Luo — Services Society, USA

Operation Committee

Jing Zeng — China Gridcom Co., Ltd., China
Yishuang Ning — Tsinghua University, China
Sheng He — Kingdee International Software Group Co., Ltd., China
Zhuolin Mei — Jiujiang University, China

Steering Committee

Calton Pu (Co-chair) — Georgia Tech, USA
Liang-Jie Zhang (Co-chair) — Shenzhen University, China

ICIOT 2025 Program Committee

Shunli Zhang	Jiujiang University, China
Abdul Mateen Ahmed	IITH, India
S. Kannadhasan	Study World College of Engineering, India
Zhuolin Mei	Jiujiang University, China
T. Nadana Ravishankar	SRM Institute of Science and Technology, India
Rafee Al Ahsan	University of Calgary, Canada
Abhishek Chanda	Cloudflare, USA
Prakash Meena	Government Engineering College Ajmer, India
Asep Wahyudin Purnomo	Universitas Gadjah Mada, Indonesia
Giuseppe Raffa	Intel Corporation, USA
Anupama B. S.	Siddaganga Institute of Technology, India
Karla Maria Ronquillo Gonzalez	Universidad Tecnológica de Chihuahua, Mexico
Ying Mei Leong	Quest International University, Malaysia
Xiaohu Fan	Wuhan Collage, China
Jaydip Sen	Praxis Business School, India
Hyuk-Yoon Kwon	Seoul National University of Science & Technology, South Korea
Young-Kyoon Suh	Kyungpook National University, South Korea

Conference Sponsor – Services Society

The Services Society (S2) is a non-profit professional organization that has been created to promote worldwide research and technical collaboration in services innovations among academia and industrial professionals. Its members are volunteers from industry and academia with common interests. S2 is registered in the USA as a "501(c) organization", which means that it is an American tax-exempt nonprofit organization. S2 collaborates with other professional organizations to sponsor or co-sponsor conferences and to promote an effective services curriculum in colleges and universities. S2 initiates and promotes a "Services University" program worldwide to bridge the gap between industrial needs and university instruction.

The Services Sector accounted for 79.5% of the GDP of the USA in 2016. The Services Society has formed 5 Special Interest Groups (SIGs) to support technology- and domain-specific professional activities.

- Special Interest Group on Services Computing (SIG-SC)
- Special Interest Group on Big Data (SIG-BD)
- Special Interest Group on Cloud Computing (SIG-CLOUD)
- Special Interest Group on Artificial Intelligence (SIG-AI)
- Special Interest Group on Metaverse (SIG-Metaverse)

About the Services Conference Federation (SCF)

As the founding member of the Services Conference Federation (SCF), the first **International Conference on Web Services (ICWS)** was held in June 2003 in Las Vegas, USA. Meanwhile, the First International Conference on Web Services - Europe 2003 (ICWS-Europe 2003) was held in Germany in October 2003. ICWS-Europe 2003 was an extended event of the 2003 International Conference on Web Services (ICWS 2003) in Europe. In 2004, ICWS-Europe was changed to the European Conference on Web Services (ECOWS), which was held in Erfurt, Germany.

Sponsored by the Services Society and Springer, SCF 2018 and SCF 2019 were held successfully on June 25 – June 30, 2018, in Seattle, USA, and on June 25 – June 30, 2019, in San Diego, USA. SCF 2020 and SCF 2021 were held successfully online and in satellite sessions in Shenzhen, China. SCF 2022 and 2023 were held successfully on December 10–14, 2022 and on September 23–26, 2023, in Hawaii, USA. SCF 2024 was held successfully on November 16–19, 2024, in Bangkok, Thailand. To celebrate its 23rd birthday, SCF 2025 was held on September 27–30, 2025, in Hong Kong, China.

In the past 22 years, the ICWS community has expanded from Web engineering innovations to scientific research for the whole services industry. Service delivery platforms have been expanded to mobile platforms, the Internet of Things, cloud computing, and edge computing. The services ecosystem has gradually been enabled, value-added, and intelligence embedded through enabling technologies such as big data, artificial intelligence, and cognitive computing. In the coming years, all transactions with multiple parties involved will be transformed into blockchain and metaverse.

Based on technology trends and best practices in the field, the Services Conference Federation (SCF) will continue serving as the conference umbrella's code name for all services-related conferences. SCF 2025 defined the future of New ABCDE (AI, Blockchain, Cloud, BigData, & IOT) and entered the 5G for Services Era. **The theme of SCF 2025 was Services Agent.** We are very proud to announce that SCF 2025's 10 co-located theme topic conferences all centered around "services", with each focusing on exploring different themes (web-based services, cloud-based services, Big Data-based services, services innovation lifecycle, AI-driven ubiquitous services, blockchain-driven trust service ecosystems, industry-specific services and applications, and emerging service-oriented technologies).

- **Bigger Platform:** The 10 collocated conferences (SCF 2025) were sponsored by the Services Society, which is the world-leading not-for-profit organization (501(c)(3)) dedicated to the service of more than 30,000 worldwide Services Computing researchers and practitioners. A bigger platform means bigger opportunities for all volunteers, authors, and participants. Meanwhile, Springer provided sponsorship of the best paper awards and other professional activities. All the 10 conference proceedings of SCF 2025 were published by Springer and indexed in the ISI Conference Proceedings Citation Index (included in Web of Science), Engineering Index EI (Compendex and Inspec databases), DBLP, Google Scholar, IO-Port, MathSciNet, Scopus, and ZBlMath.
- **Brighter Future:** While celebrating the 2025 version of ICWS, SCF 2025 highlighted the International Conference on AI and Multimodal Services (AIMS 2025) to build

the fundamental infrastructure for enabling AIGC services ecosystems. It will also lead our community members to create their own brighter future.
- **Better Model:** SCF 2025 continued to leverage the invented Conference Blockchain Model (CBM) to innovate the organizing practices for all the 10 theme conferences. Senior researchers in the field are welcome to submit proposals to serve as CBM Ambassador for an individual conference to start better interactions during your leadership role in organizing future SCF conferences.

We look forward to your great contributions as a volunteer, author, and conference participant for the fast-growing worldwide services innovations community. If you would like to contribute to SCF 2026 as a leading volunteer or try the new Conference Blockchain Model, please feel free to contact us to become a conference volunteer. For other queries or questions, please feel free to visit our conference websites and find contact information on SCF 2026.

All the invited talks and paper presentations of SCF 2020, SCF 2021, and SCF 2022 are open to all Services Society community members for free. You can watch all presentations through SCF 365.

Contents

Design and Implementation of a Software Architecture for Portable
Recording Equipment for Power Supply Service 1
   *Xiaorong He, Changhu Liang, Mingfeng Shi, Bing Shi, Yuke Zhao,
Lijuan Yao, and Jun Yang*

Auto Adaptive Fuzzy Logic Powered IoT Phishing Detection Engine 15
   Aadya Srivastava

Intelligent Analytics from Wearable Flexible Sensors for Next-Generation
Health Diagnostics 34
   Xufu Xiang, Weifang Li, Xiaotao Lin, Gang Wang, and Chungen Qian

Research and Implementation of Power Line Fault Diagnosis Technology
Based on Wavelet Transform 45
   *Mingfeng Shi, Yuke Zhao, Feifei Liu, Baolei Jia, Gaowu Huang,
and Jie Shui*

DMoE: A Semantic-Aware Engine with Mixture of Experts for Detecting
Zero-Day Malware 55
   Chenming Yang and Kejiang Ye

Research on the Bidding Game Model of Clean Energy Power in Qinghai
Evolution Province Based on Phased Network 73
   Wen Yanyan, Zhang Jisheng, and Wang Baoqi

Constructing the Data Factor Market Ecosystem: Pathways
and Mechanisms 81
   Hui Jiang, Dashan Liu, and Mengjiao Wang

Exploring the Construction of Training Communities: A Case Study
of the Smart City Management Technology Major 91
   Zhu Xiangbo

Author Index 105

Design and Implementation of a Software Architecture for Portable Recording Equipment for Power Supply Service

Xiaorong He, Changhu Liang, Mingfeng Shi[✉], Bing Shi, Yuke Zhao, Lijuan Yao, and Jun Yang

China Gridcom Co., Ltd., Shenzhen 518109, China
shimingfeng@sgchip.sgcc.com.cn

Abstract. Based on the current status of service recording in the power industry, this study analyzes the necessity of research on software architectures for Portable Recording Equipment for Power Supply Service (PREPSS). A MVVM pattern-based software architecture for PREPSS is proposed. The research was conducted through requirements analysis, overall architecture design, functional module design, and database design. An intelligent PREPSS was implemented using this architecture. Through comprehensive testing and analysis, the feasibility of the software architecture was validated. This approach provides a novel solution for service recording in the power industry, thereby enhancing the level of power supply service management.

Keywords: Portable Recording Equipment for Power Supply Service (PREPSS) · Software Architecture · MVVM Pattern · Functional Module

1 Introduction

With the advancement of society and technology, the power industry plays a vital role in the national economy, where its service quality directly impacts social stability and sustainable economic development. Every phase of power services, from electricity generation, transmission, and distribution to end-user services, requires detailed documentation of relevant business processes, service activities, and on-site conditions. These records not only serve as critical foundations for power enterprises in quality control, internal management, and performance evaluation but also act as key evidence for safeguarding customer rights and resolving service disputes [1, 2]. Traditional methods of recording power supply services suffer from multiple drawbacks: manual documentation is prone to errors and omissions; paper-based records are inconvenient to preserve and susceptible to damage or loss; and data retrieval and sharing remain challenging. In light of these limitations, research into intelligent Portable Recording Equipment for Power Supply Service (PREPSS) is urgently needed.

In China, with the continuous advancement of power system reform and rapid innovation in information technology, the Portable Recording Equipment for Power Supply

Service (PREPSS) has achieved groundbreaking results in both research and application by drawing on the design concepts and technical architectures of portable recording equipment for law enforcement [3–5]. Nevertheless, current research still exhibits several shortcomings. Some PREPSS software solutions feature incomplete functionalities, particularly inadequate capabilities in intelligent data analysis and mining, which prevents full utilization of recorded data and limits stronger support for service quality improvement.

This study aims to design and implement the software for Portable Recording Equipment for Power Supply Service (PREPSS). Through in-depth research on its architectural design and functional implementation, it is expected to provide new solutions for service recording in the power industry. On one hand, the software enables full-process recording of power supply services, including on-site operations and customer interactions, providing comprehensive and accurate data support for subsequent service quality evaluation and troubleshooting. On the other hand, equipped with smart portable IoT edge systems [6], the software leverages intelligent data analysis to detect service delivery issues in real time, enabling data-driven process optimization and quality enhancement.

2 Requirements Analysis

2.1 Functional Requirements

The Portable Recording Equipment for Power Supply Service (PREPSS) is equipped with the following basic functions video recording, photo capture, audio recording, operation prompts and status indication, synchronized audio-video recording, parameter configuration, clock function, information overlay, log recording, data storage, data protection, information interaction, video encoding, anti-shake and shock absorption, night vision capability, BeiDou positioning, key file marking, file encryption, and lighting function. Additionally, it supports optional advanced features including viewfinder preview, audio-video pre-recording, local browsing, search and playback, wireless transmission, group intercom, one-touch switching, safety risk assessment, on-site risk alert, remote real-time monitoring, remote video communication, real-time dispatching, and one-touch alarm functionality.

2.2 Performance Requirements

1. Startup Time

The system shall enter viewfinder preview mode within ≤ 30 s after pressing the power button.

2. Field of View (FOV)

The camera shall have a diagonal field of view $\geq 120°$ to ensure wide-angle coverage.

3. Wide Dynamic Range (WDR)

The device shall support WDR functionality with a dynamic range ≥ 70 dB for high-contrast scenarios.

4. Geometric Distortion

Recorded videos shall exhibit $\leq 15\%$ geometric distortion.

5. Color Reproduction

The device shall achieve accurate color reproduction. All colors on a standard color reproduction test chart must be reproducible, with the color difference (Delta E, ΔE) in the CIE LAB color space ≤ 15 for each color.

6. Video Performance

Maximum recording resolution: $\geq 2560 \times 1440$

Video frame rate: ≥ 25 fps.

Video resolution power: ≥ 800 TVL.

7. Photo Resolution

Captured images shall resolve ≥ 1000 TVL to ensure detail clarity.

8. Audio Quality

Playback audio shall be clear and continuous without noticeable stuttering or distortion.

The average harmonic distortion in human vocal range (300 Hz ~ 3 kHz) shall be $\leq 20\%$.

9. Maximum Recording Interval

In auto-segmented recording mode, the interval between consecutive recordings shall be ≤ 100 ms to ensure data continuity.

10. Display Brightness

When displaying full-field white test signal in playback mode, the screen luminance shall be ≥ 260 cd/m^2.

11. Contrast Ratio

The contrast ratio between full-white and full-black test signals in playback mode shall be $\geq 400:1$.

2.3 Security Requirements

For the Portable Recording Equipment for Power Supply Service (PREPSS), business data exchange with collection devices and field operation APPs can only be conducted after successful identity authentication and during the authenticated session. The identity authentication shall support both active and passive invalidation mechanisms. Once the identity authentication becomes invalid, the system shall immediately reject any business data exchange operations.

The Portable Recording Equipment for Power Supply Service (PREPSS) shall support secure transmission functions. When external devices access the audio-video data of PREPSS, the validity of MAC data must be verified. When external devices control PREPSS, the transmission shall use ciphertext with a Message Authentication Code (MAC).

3 Overall Architecture Design

The software of Portable Recording Equipment for Power Supply (PREPSS) adopts the MVVM (Model-View-ViewModel) architecture pattern, which can effectively separate business logic from user interface (UI), improve the testability and maintainability of code, and make the software more efficient and flexible in the development and maintenance process. The MVVM architecture consists of three parts: Model, View and ViewModel [7, 8]. The specific software architecture is shown in Fig. 1. The integration of MVVM with embedded systems offers several advantages: decoupling hardware and software to facilitate hardware iterations; lightweight data binding to reduce redundant code and resource consumption; modular design to enhance reusability and testing efficiency; centralized state management to simplify real-time control and meet to embedded requirements.

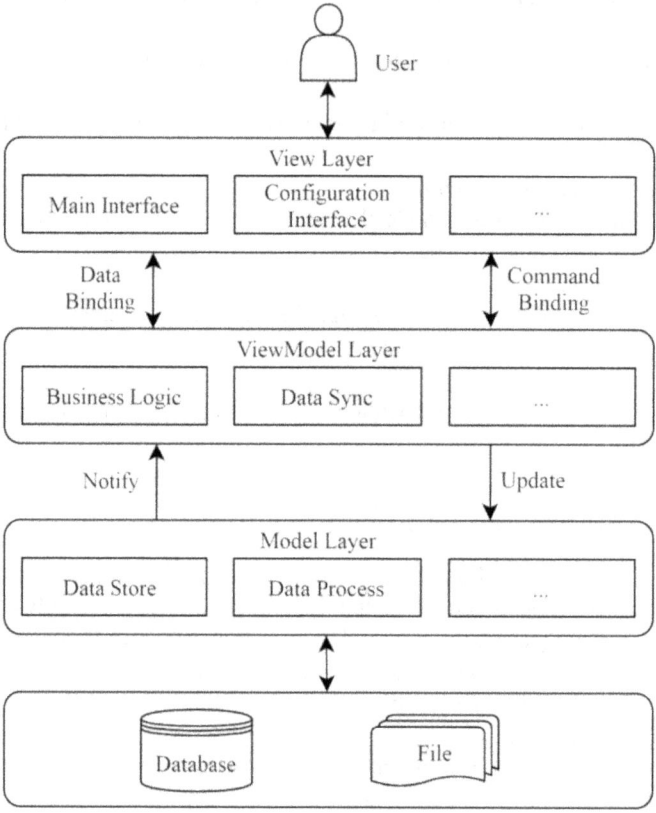

Fig. 1. Software Architecture Diagram

The Model layer is responsible for data storage and analysis tasks, utilizing Data Access Object (DAO) classes to interact with the database and perform CRUD (Create, Read, Update, Delete) operations. Through DAO classes, data such as service records and user information can be stored in a SQLite database and retrieved when needed. Additionally, the Model layer includes business logic processing classes for data manipulation and transformation, such as encoding collected audio and video data to facilitate storage and transmission.

The ViewModel layer acts as a bridge connecting the Model layer and the View layer. It handles data transfer and business logic between the View and Model layers, exposing data from the Model layer to the View layer and processing user interactions from the View layer [9].

The core functions of the View layer are user interface presentation and interaction handling, which are responsible for both receiving user input instructions and performing data visualization tasks. This layer includes modules such as the main interface, configuration interface, and recording interface. The main interface provides the core function menu of the software, supporting operation entrances for audio-video recording, photo capture, data query, etc. The configuration interface allows users to set system parameters, such as adjusting storage paths and configuring network connections. The recording interface displays real-time audio-video capture screens and integrates operation controls such as recording start/stop.

The View layer establishes bidirectional communication with the ViewModel layer through data-binding and command-binding mechanisms, enabling synchronized updates. When user input or state changes occur in the View layer, corresponding data is instantly propagated to the ViewModel. Conversely, data updates in the ViewModel automatically trigger UI re-rendering in the View layer.

4 Functional Module Design

The functional module design of the Portable Recording Equipment for Power Supply (PREPSS) software serves as the core foundation for implementing all software capabilities. Through collaborative operation, these modules collectively address the diversified needs of power supply service scenarios. The software's functional module architecture is illustrated in Fig. 2. The following sections will provide detailed introductions to core functional modules including Audio-Video Recording Module, Data Storage Module and AI-Based Intelligent Recognition Module.

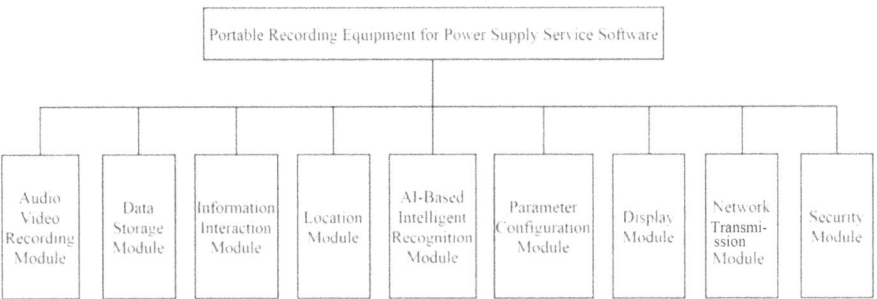

Fig. 2. Functional Module Block Diagram

4.1 Audio-Video Recording Module

The Audio-Video Recording Module undertakes the important task of collecting audio-video information at the power supply service site, providing original data support for subsequent service recording and analysis. The module mainly includes functions such as video capture, audio capture, recording control, and photo capture.

The video capture function records on-site images through the camera of the PREPSS. The specific process is shown in Fig. 3. First, the video device is initialized. During this phase, parameters such as camera resolution, frame rate, and focus mode are configured according to the device's hardware specifications and user-defined settings. Subsequently, the system enters a loop to continuously read the video stream in real-time, performing preprocessing operations such as grayscale conversion and noise reduction. The captured video frames are then cached to facilitate subsequent encoding and storage. Notably, critical information such as timestamp, location, device ID, work order number, and unit name is automatically overlaid on the recorded video to ensure data integrity and traceability.

To ensure the smoothness and stability of the video, the module will monitor the working status of the camera in real time. When an abnormal situation occurs (such as the camera being occupied or excessive device jitter), corresponding measures will be taken promptly, such as prompting the user to restart the camera or adjust the device position.

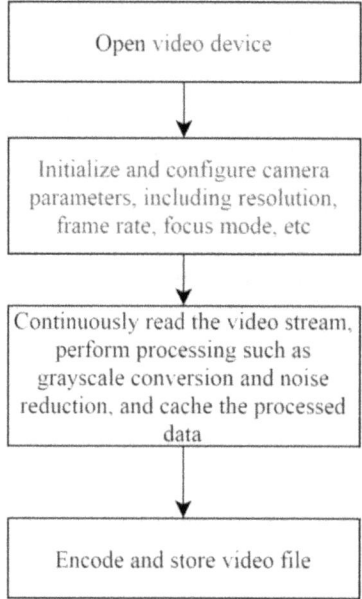

Fig. 3. Video Capture Flowchart

The audio capture function picks up on-site sounds through the microphone of the PREPSS. The specific capture process is shown in Fig. 4. First, the microphone device is activated, and parameters such as the microphone's sampling rate, number of channels, and audio format are configured during the initialization phase. Audio data is collected continuously in a loop. Processing steps like noise reduction and gain adjustment are applied to ensure clear and intelligible audio. The collected audio data is then cached according to the set format and parameters.

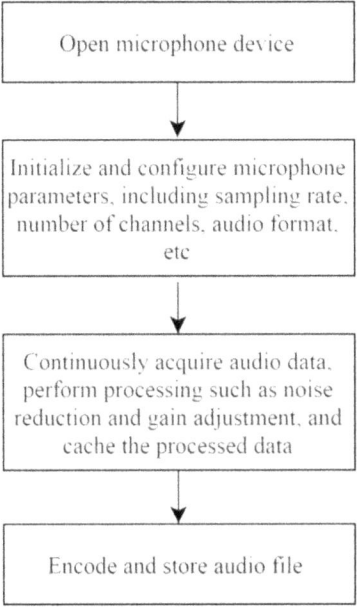

Fig. 4. Audio Capture Flowchart

The recording control function, as the core of the audio-video recording module, assumes the responsibility of managing the video and audio recording process. Users can trigger the start or stop of recording through the recording button of the PREPSS. When the user presses the recording button, the system will create a recording task, simultaneously start the video capture and audio capture threads to ensure synchronous collection of audio and video signals, thus guaranteeing the spatio-temporal consistency of subsequent data. After clicking the stop button, the module will terminate the audio-video capture threads, perform encoding, compression, and format encapsulation on the cached audio-video data to generate a complete audio-video file, and complete storage according to the preset path.

4.2 Data Storage Module

The data storage module is responsible for the secure and reliable storage of collected audio-video data, photos, text information, system configuration information, and other relevant data. The module is equipped with strict data protection mechanisms. In terms of operational permission control, operations such as deleting or modifying stored data are prohibited to ensure the integrity of original data. For abnormal scenario protection, when encountering abnormal conditions such as strong vibration, drop, forced shutdown, or power failure, the module must ensure that the recorded data is not lost or damaged.

It enhances data risk resistance through technical means such as redundant storage and real-time verification.

In the design of the local storage solution, a hybrid storage architecture of "SQLite database + file system" is adopted. For structured data, the SQLite database is used for storage. The SQLite database has the advantages of being lightweight, low in resource consumption, and simple to operate, making it very suitable for use on mobile devices. For unstructured data such as audio-video files and photos, a file storage architecture is adopted to achieve classified management. According to the data type (such as video, audio, photo) and business scenarios (such as daily inspection, fault handling, customer service, etc.), multi-level folders are created under the storage path for classified storage. The naming rule of "timestamp + service ID" combination is adopted to ensure the uniqueness and traceability of files. A file metadata index table is established in the SQLite database to record information such as file path, creation time, and affiliated service ID, realizing associated query of unstructured data and structured metadata, and further strengthening data management capabilities. To ensure data security, audio-video files are protected by the AES encryption algorithm. The exported audio-video files cannot be played without decryption, and the recorded audio-video files cannot be deleted or tampered with.

Cloud storage involves backing up data to remote servers to prevent local data loss or damage. After local data storage is completed, the data storage module executes data synchronization to cloud servers based on user-preset configurations and the current network status. The process supports both automatic triggering and manual initiation, intelligently selecting synchronization strategies (such as full synchronization or incremental synchronization) according to factors like network bandwidth and data volume, ensuring efficient and reliable consistent updates between local and cloud data.

4.3 AI-Based Intelligent Recognition Module

The AI-Based intelligent recognition module relies on artificial intelligence technology to carry out analysis and recognition of collected audio-video and image data. Its functions mainly include image recognition, speech recognition, and anomaly detection.

Specifically, this module has the function of real-time monitoring and analysis of on-site work safety risks. Safety risk assessment items include whether safety helmets are correctly worn, whether gloves are worn, etc. When on-site safety risks are identified, voice broadcast alarm prompts are issued. The process is shown in Fig. 5. First, preprocessing operations are performed on the original image, specifically including image size scaling, color space conversion (such as RGB to grayscale), and data normalization to optimize image quality and adapt to model input requirements. Then, the preprocessed image is input into a pre-trained detection model for target detection and classification. Finally, feature recognition and logical judgment are carried out, and voice alarms are broadcast for those who do not wear safety helmets or gloves.

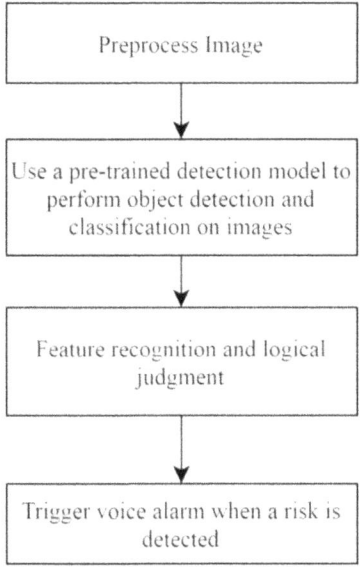

Fig. 5. Safety Risk Assessment Flowchart

5 Database Design

Database design is a critical component of the Portable Recording Equipment for Power Supply Service (PREPSS) software design, and its rationality directly affects data storage efficiency, query speed, and management security. For structured data, a SQLite database is adopted for storage, and core data tables such as service record table, audio-video record table, and location information record table are designed to meet diverse data storage and query requirements. The details of each table are shown in Tables 1 to 3.

Table 1. Service Record Table

Field Name	Data Type	Primary Key	Description
service_id	INTEGER	YES	Power supply service ID
service_time	DATETIME	NO	Power supply service time
work_order_no	TEXT	NO	Work order number
manage_unit	TEXT	NO	Power supply management unit
service_personnel_no	TEXT	NO	Power service personnel number
customer_no	TEXT	NO	Power customer number
photo_file_path	TEXT	NO	Photo file storage path
audio_file_path	TEXT	NO	Audio file storage path
video_file_path	TEXT	NO	Video file storage path
position_info_file_path	TEXT	NO	Position information file storage path

Table 2. Audio-Video Record Table

Field Name	Data Type	Primary Key	Description
video_file_path	TEXT	YES	Photo/Audio/Video file storage path
file_save_time	DATETIME	NO	File storage time
service_id	INTEGER	NO	Power supply service ID

Table 3. Position Information Record Table

Field Name	Data Type	Primary Key	Description
position_info_file_path	TEXT	YES	Position information file storage path
file_save_time	DATETIME	NO	File storage time
service_id	INTEGER	NO	Power supply service ID

6 Test Verification and Analysis

To verify the feasibility of the software architecture for the Portable Recording Equipment for Power Supply Service (PREPSS), an intelligent version of the PREPSS was developed based on this architecture, and testing and verification were carried out. The test plan covers 33 experimental items, including 19 functional tests and 14 performance tests. After comprehensive testing, all items met the design requirements, verifying the effectiveness and reliability of the software architecture (Table 4).

Table 4. Test Items

Serial No	Functional Test Items	Performance Test Items
1	Video Recording Test	Startup Time Test
2	Photo Capture Test	Field of View Test
3	Audio Recording Test	Wide Dynamic Range Test
4	Operation Prompt and Status Indication Test	Geometric Distortion Test
5	Audio-Video Synchronous Recording Test	Color Reproduction Test
6	Parameter Configuration Test	Video Performance Test
7	Clock Function Test	Photo Resolution Test
8	Information Overlay Test	Audio Quality Test
9	Log Recording Test	Maximum Recording Interval Test

(*continued*)

Table 4. (*continued*)

Serial No	Functional Test Items	Performance Test Items
10	Data Storage Test	Display Brightness Test
11	Data Protection Test	Contrast Ratio Test
12	Information Interaction Test	CPU Load
13	Anti-Shake and Shock Absorption Test	Memory Usage
14	Night Vision Function Test	Battery Consumption
15	BeiDou Positioning Function Test	–
16	Key File Marking Test	–
17	File Encryption Test	–
18	Lighting Function Test	–
19	Safety Risk Assessment Test	–

Given the page limit constraints of the paper, this study focuses on two functional tests and one performance test for detailed analysis.

6.1 Audio-Video Synchronous Recording Test

The test sample shall continuously record for 4 h. At least five points (including file start and end) within the recorded files shall be randomly selected for synchronized playback evaluation. Audio-video synchronization during playback shall be comprehensively evaluated through visual and auditory inspection. During recording, the digital audio shall not have obvious lag or lead relative to the video image. During playback of any segment, the audio-video out-of-sync time shall not exceed 1 s. Any occurrence of out-of-sync exceeding this threshold and its duration shall be recorded (Table 5).

Table 5. Audio-Video Synchronous Recording Test Results

Serial No	Test items	Number of tests	Number of Passed Tests	Pass Rate
1	Audio-Video Synchronous Recording Test	10 times	10 times	100%

Experimental data analysis shows that the audio-video synchronous recording function meets the standard requirements.

6.2 Safety Risk Assessment Test

First, carry out test preparation, including one Portable Recording Equipment for Power Supply Service (PREPSS), safety helmets of various colors, toy caps, red buckets, and 10 test personnel of different ages, genders, and heights, to simulate different indoor and outdoor scenarios, which can cover test samples of different personnel, wearing states, and lighting conditions. During the test execution process, first conduct basic function tests to verify the system's basic recognition capabilities, then carry out complex scenario tests to simulate interference factors in real environments, and finally implement boundary condition tests to address extreme situations. At the same time, detailed records shall be kept of the scenario settings, personnel operation status, system output results, etc., for each test, and key indicators such as accuracy rate, false alarm and miss rate, and response time shall be analyzed.

1. Basic Function Test

In a simple scenario with fixed lighting and unobstructed views, instruct test personnel to sequentially pass through the camera's field of view while wearing compliant safety helmets, and then while not wearing safety helmets.

2. Complex Scenario Test

Scenario 1: Lighting Variation

The lighting intensity settings cover four typical lighting conditions: high-intensity light (e.g., direct sunlight at noon outdoors), low-light (e.g., dim indoor lighting, low-light environment at dusk), backlight (where the tester's face or head is backlit when facing away from the light source), and nighttime (with only artificial supplementary lighting). During the test, testers are required to repeat the actions of "wearing/non-wearing" safety helmets in each lighting environment and sequentially pass through the camera's field of view.

Scenario 2: Occlusion and Background Interference

In scenarios where the tester's head is partially occluded (e.g., face or head blocked by handheld tools), the tester is required to repeatedly perform the actions of "wearing/non-wearing" designated items and pass through the camera's field of view. In the background, objects similar to safety helmets (such as red buckets) are placed to observe whether the device misjudges due to interfering objects.

Scenario 3: Dynamics and Multi-angle

Firstly, simulate personnel in fast-moving states, including different movement speeds such as walking and running. Secondly, adjust the camera shooting angles, capturing testers performing "wearing/non-wearing" actions from top-down, side, and upward views, to verify the system's recognition capability in complex dynamic environments.

3. Boundary Condition Test

The test covers three typical scenarios: safety helmets with colors highly similar to the background (e.g., white safety helmets in front of white walls), personnel wearing non-standard safety helmets (such as toy caps), and multi-person scenarios where multiple individuals appear in the same frame (Table 6).

Table 6. Security Risk Assessment Test Results

Serial No	Test items	Number of tests	Number of Passed Tests	Pass Rate
1	Basic Function Test	200 times	196 times	98%
2	Complex Scenario Test	200 times	185 times	92.5%
3	Boundary Condition Test	200 times	180 times	90%

Experimental data analysis shows that the Portable Recording Equipment for Power Supply Service (PREPSS) can effectively identify the behavior of not wearing safety helmets in various test scenarios, realizing safety risk assessment and early warning functions, with a recognition success rate exceeding 90%.

6.3 Video Performance Test

1. Video Resolution Test

For the resolution test, continuously capture the ISO 12233 resolution test chart for 1 min. Subsequently, import the recorded video file into image quality analysis software to calculate the video resolution value, which shall not be lower than 2560 × 1440.

2. Video Frame Rate Test

For the frame rate test, use image quality analysis software to perform single-frame playback and testing on the output video signal. The video frame rate shall be not less than 25 frames per second (fps).

3. Video Resolving Power Test

Capture the ISO 12233 resolution test chart, and use image quality analysis software to calculate the resolving power of the sampled video frames. The video resolving power shall be not less than 800 TVL (Table 7).

Table 7. Video Performance Test Results

Serial No	Test items	Number of tests	Number of Passed Tests	Pass Rate
1	Video Resolution Test	100 times	100 times	100%
2	Video Frame Rate Test	100 times	100 times	100%
3	Video Resolving Power Test	100 times	100 times	100%

Experimental data analysis shows that the video resolution, video frame rate, and video resolving power meet the standard requirements.

7 Conclusions

This paper designs the software architecture for the Portable Recording Equipment for Power Supply Service (PREPSS). First, a requirements analysis is conducted, and based on this analysis, the overall architecture design is carried out by adopting the MVVM architectural pattern, which separates business logic from view presentation, effectively improving code maintainability and testability. Then, functional module design is performed according to the software functions of the PREPSS, introducing the main functional modules. Finally, experiments verify that the software meets the technical requirements related to the software. According to the experimental results, the software design architecture proposed in this paper has strong feasibility and practicality, capable of meeting the functional and performance requirements of the PREPSS, providing strong technical support for the power supply services of power enterprises.

References

1. Peng, H., Zheng, M.: Research on the management innovation of electric power enterprises. Manag. Technol. SME **3**(07), 14–15 (2019)
2. Tian, L.: A brief analysis of the promotion and innovation of high-quality services in power marketing. Electric Power Syst. Equip. (08), 174–176 (2022)
3. Fan, P., Shen, J.: Research on command and dispatch support application of portable recording equipment for law enforcement in mobile internet Era. In: Proceedings of the 2019 National Academic Symposium on Public Security Communications (Excellent Papers), pp. 181–185 (2019)
4. Zhao, G., Chen, J., Zheng, H., et al.: Research on anti-shake algorithm of portable recording equipment for law enforcement. Embedded Technol. **49**(04), 98–104 (2023)
5. Zhang, T.: Research on the application of intelligent speech technology on portable recording equipment for law enforcement. China Public Secur. (Academy Edi) (02), 125–129 (2019)
6. Tong, J., Qi, Z., Pu, T., et al.: Edge intelligence to power Internet of Things: concept, architecture, technology and application. Proc. CSEE **44**(14), 5473–5495 (2024)
7. Chen, T.: MVVM design pattern and its application. Comput. Digital Eng. **42**(10), 1982–1985 (2014)
8. Ke, X., Zhou, C.: Development of stem analysis information management system based on MVVM architecture. Forest Eng. **37**(01), 18–27 (2021)
9. Cui, H.: The application of MVVM mode in android project. China Comput. Commun. **33**(06), 1–3 (2021)

Auto Adaptive Fuzzy Logic Powered IoT Phishing Detection Engine

Aadya Srivastava(✉)

Cambridge Center for International Research (CCIR), Milton, UK
aadya.s@icloud.com

Abstract. Phishing is the most common precursor for an Internet of Things (IoT) targeting attack. To curtail attacks, malware and web browser detection engines, similar to other research studies, rely on publicly available past-performance datasets and crowd sourcing to train their internal algorithms. This generic implementation ensures that their relevance declines over time as cyber-attacks gain sophistication and eventually become harder to detect. This study detects phishing webpages with an accuracy rate of >97% (AUC ≈ 0.97 – 1.0) via dynamically derived features and weights generated using Classification Based on Association (CBA). This study commenced with static model analysis where Fuzzy Logic (FL) generated an AUC of 1.0. However, this would overfit due to old patterns and the rate of detection eventually declines by 15% over time to an AUC of 0.85–0.90. The study was updated to deploy data drift analysis to detect significant degradation (>5%) which eventually occurred due evolving phishing patterns. This led to the development of an adaptive (or auto-updating) FL system which used regenerated (or adapted) features, weights, rules and other FL aspects ensuring an AUC ≈ 0.97 – 1.0. These adapted features and weights were fed back into model and confirmed post verification of improvement in detection ratios. This ensured that this model could be left unattended while the adaptive data drift did not deviate, underscoring the importance of data-driven feature tuning in maintaining detection efficacy in evolving threat landscapes. The study uncovered existing and novel attacks that deployed authorization tokens and not login forms to gain access.

Keywords: Automated Phishing Detection · Fuzzy Logic · Adaptive Learning

1 Introduction

Internet of Things (IoT) has seen rapid technological advancement, however IoT device security remains a critical concern [1] as poorly tested security measures have led to a rise in attacks and threatens the growth of IoT device deployment [2]. Manufacturers are struggling with an unprecedented demand of IoT which forces them to rely on churning out via production lines while overlooking security. The global coverage of IoT technology makes it susceptible to cyberattacks owing to campaigns that steal sensitive information, and cause substantial economic damage [3].

Phishing is the leading infection vector [4] that socially engineer's users via a maliciously crafted login page, link, or file into divulging corporate or personal login information to initiate a ransomware, malware, data-breach, or other attacks. Phishing dominates 90% [5] of mobile and 87% of desktop attacks [6] which originates from over 3 billion [4] spoofed (or phishing) emails a day. These attacks are responsible for US$2.9 billion dollars in losses in the U.S. according to the FBI's Internet Crime Complaint Centre [7, 8] (IC3, 2023) and amount to $9 billion annually [9] or a staggering US$17,700 per minute. Phishing email are the 'attack of choice' as they represent a low-cost and easy method to target an organisation or a network.

This study uses Fuzzy Logic (FL) to detect 'Google Mail (or Gmail)', 'Proton Mail', and 'Yahoo! Mail' phishing pages across the internet and can be extended to detect service such as login pages for CCTV, Scada, and other IoT/industrial systems. This study commenced with email phishing attacks owing to Gmail's status of the world's largest [10] email provider combined with Google's ownership [11] of Chrome browser. We assumed that the browser will have an in-built priority to detect attacks against their own infrastructure and wanted to test our FL research against a protected system without using training data. However, we detected hundreds of phishing pages that we were accessible on Chrome in addition to other popular browsers such as Safari and Mozilla. To counter this glaring vulnerability our research built an open-source and free-to-use platform that passively scans the internet's backbone to detect malicious pages. This platform or Server Security Project (SSP) has a FL engine that surpasses the heuristics detection algorithms of web-browsers and other online protection suites to detect advanced and up-to-date phishing techniques. SSP once trained, uses current phishing attack's features to auto-upgrade its core which reduce reliance on third-party datasets. This ensures SSP's relevance over time as it continues to detect the latest and sophisticated attacks without waiting for a third-party to release a dataset. Hence, SSP is a truly self-sufficient auto-adaptive platform that scans the full spectrum of IPv4 and IPv6 to detect and assist in blocking phishing infrastructure that may lead to network compromise, data-leaks, ransomware, and devastating malware installations. Thus, SSP ensures that internet security is enhanced while protecting the most vulnerable, yet underfunded, organisations vital towards the functioning of a society.

2 Literature Review

This paper analyses several studies but it is important to highlight an FL study by Aburros et al. [12] that served as an inspiration to create new filters/layers, new features, and incorporate real world/live datasets for training and analysis. This early paper proposed a FL-based classifier to detect phishing websites by static extracted features and applied fuzzy rules to generate phishing probability scores. The fuzzy inference system was based on a Sugeno-type model and was trained using expert-defined rules. The dated study lacks adaptability, relies on static logic, and would struggle against today's adversarial or obfuscated phishing techniques. The study lists FL rules that were defined manually by experts rather than learned from data thus, introduced human bias and limit scalability. The study also had a 27 fixed feature set that did not incorporate real-time model update, and had limited generalization owing static rule sets and handcrafted thresholds, that could not detect new domains or novel phishing adaptations. However, this study paved the way for our modern FL engine that enabled SSP to auto-update its own features during scanning. Thus, creating a true open-source dynamic phishing detection engine.

Owing to rapid enhancements in Language Learning Models (LLM) realm, we are proposing a FL engine that surpasses current LLM models without training and a significantly lower computational cost. To build such an engine, we analysed the following LLM studies and their implementations:

Liu et al. [13] development PhishLLM, a phishing detection framework that uses LLMS (GPT-3.5) combined with OCR, CLIP (for image analysis), and fuzzy logic to classify suspicious websites. It analyzes textual and visual content of webpages, including screenshots and rendered DOMs, to detect phishing pages that evade traditional detection engines. It leverages prompting and visual-semantic embeddings to reason page content, brand impersonation, and layout similarities. PhishLLM. However, is slow as it uses OCR and LLM which needs the input of a rendered email/website by means of a screenshot limiting its real-time capability. Dependence on OpenAI and image processing APIs poses privacy, costs (GPT subscription), and deployment constraints in underfunded or secure environments.

Li et al. study [14] created a LLM driven phishing detection process called, KnowPhish. This leverages multimodal learning that combines visual, textual, and structural information to detect phishing websites with high accuracy and speed. Unlike approaches that focus on blacklists or hand-crafted rules, KnowPhish trains a multimodal LLM to detect deceptive cues in webpage layout, text content, and brand impersonation patterns. A key innovation in KnowPhish is its use of a Knowledge-Based Prior, which incorporates information about legitimate brands and website structures to aid in recognizing phishing attempts. The system processes both HTML source code and rendered screenshots enabling comparison against known legitimate brand templates. Its evaluation showed a significant speed advantage, nearly 30x faster than DynaPhish, a leading visual phishing detector. KnowPhish maintains strong detection performance, particularly against zero-day and visually sophisticated phishing pages. KnowPhish has severe limitations, its reliance on brand-specific prior knowledge means it performs poorly when encountering phishing pages that impersonate brands not present in its knowledge base. The detection accuracy is thus tightly coupled with the dataset used during training. Additionally, it is faster than many prior systems but KnowPhish is computationally intensive as it requires visual processing steps (e.g., rendering, feature fusion), impacting scalability when deployed at internet scale. Finally, the system's internals are proprietary which limits testing and third-party evaluation.

Sun et al. [15] phishing detection framework integrates Multimodal Large Language Models (MLLMs) with knowledge-based planning agents to emulate human-like decision-making in identifying phishing websites, called PhishAgent. It implements an autonomous reasoning that dynamically selects which parts of a webpage to analyze and which tools (e.g., vision models, LLMs) to use, based on the context. PhishAgent's approach is to execute goal-oriented agentic pipeline, inspired by planning-based AI Goal Execution Planning (GEP) like agents. The system processes a website by first breaking it into components (e.g., visual layout, text, domain metadata), then invokes specific model-based "skills" such as GPT-4-based reasoning, optical character recognition (OCR), or structural checks. This enables multi-turn, interactive analysis, allowing the system to ask itself follow-up questions ("Is the login form redirecting to a known brand domain?") to improve detection fidelity. PhishAgent is computationally heavy and slow, with reported inference times exceeding 10 s per webpage, making it impractical for real-time detection. The use of multiple agent "skills" (LLMs, OCR, image recognition) in a sequential pipeline adds to latency and operational complexity. PhishAgent's reliance on task planning and skill selection logic overfits with unexpected webpage designs or content obfuscation. Since it builds decisions dynamically, the reasoning varies significantly across multiple runs that makes debugging and testing very difficult. Furthermore, the system requires various third-party tools and APIs, which introduces deployment challenges, privacy concerns, and high API costs.

Chen et al.'s study [16] on phishing detection explores the small, lightweight, open-source LLM (Qwen2.5–1.5B). This approach was inspired by the need to reduce latency, memory footprint, and inference costs compared to large-scale models like GPT-3 or GPT-4. Qwen2.5–1.5B, is a compact transformer-based model that supports instruction-following and classification tasks while remaining small to run efficiently on consumer-grade GPUs. The study develops Qwen2.5–1.5B using a phishing classification that inputs the SpamAssassin dataset containing labeled examples of spam and phishing emails. The study achieved 97.6% accuracy and showcases its ability to provide equal or higher detection rates than larger models but only on domain-specific classification tasks. Its fast inference time (~1–5 ms per query) and low hardware requirements make it suitable for real-time phishing detection, particularly for secure email gateways or endpoint security solutions. Its limitation is that it only accepts text without the option to analyzing visual elements such as login forms, spoofed logos, or webpage layout. Hence, the model's scope is restricted to email while lacking detection modules for URL, SSL certificates, or heuristic cues, that are vital for phishing detection. While it can be deployed quickly, its reliance on SpamAssassin, a small dataset, limits the model's real-world applications as it needs frequent retraining.

Via detailed analysis, it was inferred that the root cause of ineffective phishing detection platforms was (a) the lack of a true real-time dataset, (b) enabling self-updating of features/tokens to ensure temporal relevance, and (c) monitoring a large spectrum of features such as, domains, text, and other elements for an effective phishing detecting engine. Hence, this study pivoted away from basic ML and tokenisation study and decided to use FL to determine if the site was a phishing vector or not.

3 Methodology

Phishing attacks are designed to duplicate a legitimate website in design, interaction(s), and activity. An attacker undertakes significant efforts to imitate key elements such as URL, syntax, form designs, and other features to trick an end user into giving up their credentials or download malicious files. As the attacks continue to evolve and achieve technical sophistication, their success rate increases especially in the corporate and personal email category. To evaluate the legitimacy of a website, an end-user needs to undertake a deep analysis of the content, context (origin link/source), and via third party datasets. In other words, phishing detection entails robust identification that is achievable only via comprehensive technical knowledge and skill.

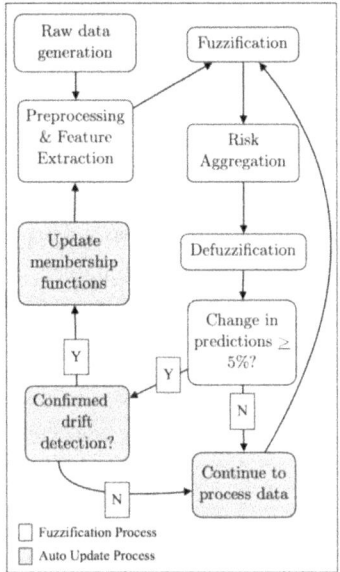

Fig. 1. Auto adaptive Fuzzy logic flowchart

This is an ideal job for data classification, FL, and computational algorithms. Figure 1 displays the process from raw generation to classification of a site as 'phishing' or 'safe' via FL and the auto-updating of feature via the process as in the grey boxes. This enables the phishing classification to be passed to the 'Feature Weight Updating' section and then proceeds to be analysed and fed back to the feature extraction for re-fuzzification. The details are included in the following sub-sections.

3.1 Raw Data Generation

SSP queries Censys to scans 100% of IPv4 and 100% of in-use IPv6 range to obtain any HTML tag or defined response within 6 to 64 kb of response. Hence, the issue with a limited dataset is has been solved in our research. To execute search for phishing sites, SSP queries to detect pages that contain the words, "Login" and "Gmail" in their title by querying the tag 'services.http.response.html_title:/Gmai[l]+/' where the colon symbol (:) indicates that the query is case sensitive and equal symbol (=) would indicate case insensitive. For Yahoo, we used 'services.http.response.html_title:/Yaho[o]+/' and for Proton, we used, 'services.http.response.html_title:/Proto[n]+/'. For the month of June 2025, we queried the IPv4 range to obtain 20,900 websites out of which SSP accurately detected 10% Gmail Phishing pages while 5% were Yahoo and Proton Mail.

3.2 Pre Processing and Feature Extraction

SSP implements a multi-dimensional assessment by automating analysis post extraction of relevant features. Through manual review of phishing sites post Classification Based on Associations (CBA) rules (Table 1) output a total of 25 quantitative threat indicators. We are deploying CBA so that this process can be truly automated when data drift is detected in the defuzzification stage. SSP utilized the dataset from Censys that consisted of real-time crawled phishing and legitimate websites with 25 Key Phishing Characteristic Indicators grouped into 4 filters and class labels: {Legitimate, Suspicious, Phishing} via the rules generated by CBA (Table 1). Instead of having filters, as commonly implemented in fuzzy logic, this study uses a layered approach where the layers are labelled as Core Layer (CL), Outer Layer #1 (OL1), Outer Layer #2 (OL2), and Auxiliary Layer (AL) as core attributes in phishing detection. The CL's nomenclature will be decided during set-up with feature sets that are unique to the particular website which is being analyzed for phishing attacks. For e.g. the text embedded within the site, the SSL information, logo colors, and other features. The other layer's nomenclature will also be decided during set up however, they can be updated by a deciding algorithm when data drift is detected. These features will be auto-enumerated using obtaining rank features on recent data and then extracting features and replacing them in the CL, OL_x, or AL as explained in Subsect. 3.8.

These indicators serve as structured input variables to our detection model, are presented in Table 2. The features within the filters were identified via Random Forest ranking to detect how much these features were contributing to reducing the error during classification. To define the features, our platform created the weights as per their probabilities in sites that were previously identified as phishing.

Weights (Table 2) can be obtained by support (how often the rule applies in the dataset) and confidence (how often the rule is correct when it applies). The feature weights for URL Length are normalized by defining the raw range between 5 to 200 characters and normalized via:

$$\text{URL}_{norm} = (\text{length} - 5)/(200 - 5) \tag{1}$$

The normalized range values near '0' indicate "Short URL" (possibly legitimate) while near '1' indicate, "Very long URL" (possibly phishing).

Given $x \in [0,1]$ as the normalized 'URL Length', is defined as:

$$\text{Short}(x) = max(0, min(1, 2 \cdot (0.5 - x))) \tag{2}$$

$$\text{Medium}(x) = max(0, 1 - \mid 2 \cdot (x - 0.5) \mid) \tag{3}$$

$$\text{Long}(x) = max(0, min(1, 2 \cdot (x - 0.5))) \tag{4}$$

A normalized value < 0.3 has 'high Short membership', and almost zero Long, a value around 0.5 will have 'peak Medium membership', and a value > 0.7 belongs to Long.

Table 1. CBA Rules to identify phishing pages

ID	Association Rule (IF… THEN)	Support (%)	Confidence (%)	Class
R1	IF URL Length = Long AND Request URL = External THEN Phishing	22.5	87.2	Phishing
R2	IF Domain Age = New AND Issuing Authority = SelfSigned THEN Phishing	18.4	89.6	Phishing
R3	IF Base URL = External AND Link Names = Obscure THEN Phishing	15.6	85.3	Phishing
R4	IF Username Input = Absent AND Password Input = Absent THEN Legitimate	20.1	91.2	Legitimate
R5	IF RGB Value = High Contrast AND Color Distribution = Skewed THEN Suspicious	10.7	78.9	Suspicious
R6	IF Cookie Values = Safe AND Abnormal Cookie = Absent THEN Legitimate	14.9	83.5	Legitimate
R7	IF NONCE = Absent AND No Follow Tag = Present THEN Phishing	9.2	75.0	Phishing
R8	IF Is SSL Used = No AND Distinguished Name = Mismatch THEN Phishing	12.8	88.1	Phishing

3.3 Fuzzification

Fuzzification is the initial stage in a FL system where crisp input values (numerical or categorical features) are transformed into fuzzy linguistic variables. This process enables the system to handle vagueness inherent in phishing detection. Input features such as URL length, SSL certificate status, domain age, and other exhibit graded severity rather than discrete labels. Fuzzification allows these features to be represented using linguistic terms (e.g., Short, Medium, Long) which can be evaluated by fuzzy inference rules. In other words, traditional binary logic makes hard decisions of yes or no (0 or 1). However, in the real-world cybersecurity 0 or 1 is not an option and crisp value (such as URL length = 85) might not be inherently malicious. A URL Length = 85 can be fuzzified as: Short: [0, 0, 50], Medium: [40, 60, 80], Long: [70, 100, 100] and represented by triangular or trapezoidal membership functions (Fig. 2).

3.4 Fuzzy Rule Base

The fuzzy rule table (rule base) for filter 1 in Table 3 is a collection of IF–THEN rules that uses our research and knowledge about what features and their combinations would result in higher or lower phishing risk.

Each rule uses the fuzzified inputs in its antecedent (IF part) and assigns a fuzzy output in the consequent (THEN part). Rules are expressed in linguistic terms and have multiple antecedents joined by fuzzy logical operators AND or OR. For example, rules for phishing detection (Table 3). Conditions such as, "URL length is Long" or "Domain age is New" refers to the fuzzy membership of the input in that set. In this case, the output

Table 2. Fuzzy Logic Feature Details

Feature	Fuzzy Terms *(Membership Function Type)*	Weight
CORE LAYER (CL): HTML RESPONSE AND URL (WEIGHT = 0.30)		
Page Title	Relevant, Irrelevant *(Similar keywords)*	10
Page Text	Original, Generic, Obfuscated *(NLP uniqueness)*	10
Username Form	Present, Absent *(Binary membership)*	10
Password Form	Present, Absent *(Binary membership)*	10
Request URL	Internal, External, Mixed *(Matching Domains)*	20
URL Length	Short, Medium, Long *(Length (Triangular)*	40
Abnormal DNS Data	Normal, Suspicious *(TTL, MX/A mismatch)*	25
OUTER LAYER #1 (OL1): PAGE SOURCE, JS, AND IMAGES (WEIGHT = 0.25)		
NONCE	Present, absent *(Security practice marker)*	5
Base URL	Checl domain, *(Cross-check registered domain)*	10
No-Follow Tag	Present, absent *(Search engine manipulation)*	5
Link Names	Descriptive, obscure *(NLP-based scoring)*	10
Link Targets	Consistent, randomized *(href pattern entropy)*	10
Link Direction	Internal, external *(Percentage-based)*	15
RGB Values	Uniform, high contrast *(Image analysis)*	20
Colour Distribution	Balanced, skewed *(Detect mimicry)*	25
OUTER LAYER #2 (OL2): DNS & LOCAL STORAGE (WEIGHT = 0.20)		
Domain Age	New, Medium, Old *(Registered days)*	25
Domain Rank	Low, Medium, High *(SimilarWeb APIs)*	20
Abnormal Cookie	Present, Absent *(Cookie behaviour anomalies)*	15

(continued)

Table 2. (*continued*)

Feature	Fuzzy Terms (Membership Function Type)	Weight
Cookie Values	Safe, Encoded, Obfuscated (Base64/token values)	15
AUXILLARY LAYER (AL): SSL & REMOTE SERVER (WEIGHT = 0.25)		
Is SSL Used?	Yes, No (Binary)	10
Issuing Authority	Trusted/untrusted/self-signed (CA lookup)	25
Distinguished Name	Matches Domain, Mismatch (Certificate check)	25
Shared/Ded. Host	Shared, Dedicated (Hosting data)	20
Same Domains Host	None, Some, Many (Suspicious hosts check)	20

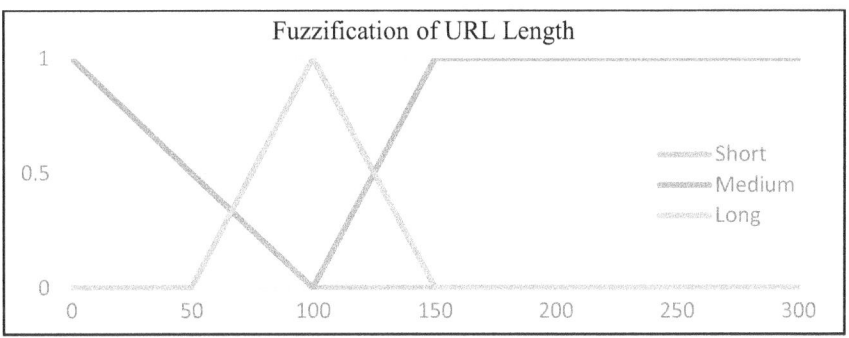

Fig. 2. Displays the fuzzification of a URL length value (85) into fuzzy sets (Short, Medium, Long) and how a crisp input maps to degrees of membership in multiple fuzzy categories.

variable 'Phishing-Risk' with fuzzy sets are defined as {Low, Medium, High} risk. For instance, Rule 1's consequent "High" would correspond to a fuzzy set (perhaps defined on a scale of 0–10 or 0–100 for risk) that represents a high likelihood of phishing. When the crisp inputs have been fuzzified and the rule base established, SSP evaluates all the rules in parallel. Rule firing determining the degree to which each fuzzy rule is satisfied by the current inputs. This involves combining the membership values from fuzzification for a majority of combinations where (a) a rule with a single condition (e.g. "IF domain age is New THEN risk is High") is allotted the value of the membership of the input, (b) rules with multiple antecedents joined by AND, are allotted the minimum operator (or sometimes the product) to the set of membership degrees. Rule 1's conditions has yielded: URL length is Long ($\mu = 0.4$), Domain age is New ($\mu = 1.0$), SSL is Invalid ($\mu = 1.0$), then with AND generate *min (0.4, 1.0, 1.0) = 0.4*. This rule would fire with strength 0.4 (40%).

Table 3. Fuzzy Rule Table for Filter 1

IF						THEN
Filter 1 Rule	Page Title	Username Input	Password Input	Request URL	URL Length	Phishing-Risk
1	Matching	Present	Present	Legitimate	Short	Low
2	Matching	Present	Present	Suspicious	Long	High
3	Mismatched	Present	Present	Suspicious	Long	High
4	Mismatched	Absent	Present	Suspicious	Medium	Medium
5	Mismatched	Absent	Absent	Suspicious	Long	High
6	Matching	Absent	Present	Legitimate	Medium	Medium
7	Mismatched	Present	Absent	Suspicious	Long	High
8	Matching	Present	Absent	Suspicious	Long	Medium
9	Matching	Absent	Absent	Legitimate	Short	Low
10	Mismatched	Present	Present	Legitimate	Long	Medium

3.5 Risk Aggregation

This step combines the outputs from multiple fuzzy layers into a single final risk score that lists the overall threat level of a given website. Each layer in the system (HTML, JavaScript, DNS, SSL, and others) produce a layer-specific fuzzy risk score of - Layer 1 (HTML & URL): 0.7 (High Risk), Layer 2 (Source & JS): 0.5 (Moderate Risk), Layer 3 (DNS & Cookies): 0.3 (Low Risk), and Layer 4 (SSL & Hosting): 0.8 (High Risk).

This is a critical step that happens after fuzzification and rule evaluation, and before defuzzification in a fuzzy logic system. Each fuzzy set defines how strongly a certain numeric output value (e.g. phishing score) belongs to a linguistic category (Low, Medium, High). The orange filled region is the result of aggregating all truncated fuzzy sets using the max (union) operator. This represents the system's combined fuzzy conclusion based on all rules.

$$\mu_{aggregated}(z) = \max(\mu_{Low}(z), \mu_{Medium}(z), \mu_{High}(z)) \tag{5}$$

Aggregation combines the outputs of all rules into a single unified fuzzy set that reflects the overall reasoning of the fuzzy inference system and becomes the input for defuzzification. The final aggregated risk score is the weighted sum of these scores.

$$Total\ Risk = \sum_{i=1}^{n} W_i.R_i \tag{6}$$

R_i = defuzzied score from layer i (range 0 to 1 or 0 to 100)
W_i = importance weight for layer i
$\sum W_i = 1$ (weights are normalised)

The weighted sum as above ensures (a) flexibility that ensures that certain features importance is defined or new items can be monitored that increase their importance with changed in cyber-attack methodology (e.g., SSL might be more important than image colour), (b) is easier to explain, and (c) enable modularity as each layer can be independently tuned without redesigning the whole system.

3.6 Defuzzification

Defuzzification is the final step in a fuzzy inference system. It converts the aggregated fuzzy output set into a single, precise crisp value suitable for decision-making or triggering actions via automated cyber security systems. The output is produced in the form of membership functions in linguistic terms (e.g., Low, Medium, High risk) or as a probability or confidence level (depending on the process chosen) to enable value driven actions such as alerting users or blocking access. To achieve the result three popular methods are available in academic realm and their analysis is:

Criteria	Centroid	MOM/LOM/SOM	Bisector
Accuracy	High	Moderate	High
Computational Cost	Moderate	Low	Moderate
Interpretability	High	Moderate	Moderate
Outlier Sensitivity	Low	High	Medium

We chose the Centroid process as it allows the best results by following this mathematical implementation:

Generate set of fuzzy output rules:

$$\mu_{High}(y) = 0.8, \mu_{Medium}(y) = 0.4 \quad (7)$$

Generate aggregated output μout(y):

$$\mu out(y) = \max(\mu High(y), \mu Medium(y)) \quad (8)$$

Centroid defuzzification is computed over the spectrum of results for Risk Score

$$\int y \cdot \mu out(y) dy / \int \mu out(y) dy \quad (9)$$

3.7 Auto Adaptive Process for Phishing Detection

The static fuzzy system, as discussed until now, appears perfect till the features do not change as it incorrectly assumes that real-world patterns do not shift. This is the misleading assumption with all previous studies. As analysis progresses with time, there is degradation in detection owing to changes in phishing techniques and eventually leads to a decline in a model's relevance. To counter, SSP monitors data drift in the current and previous result. Data drift, a change in statistical properties in input data, leads to degradation of a model's performance. In other words, the fuzzy rules, membership functions, and other inference mechanics do not match to the real-world behaviour lead to a drop in the positive outcome or detection accuracy of the model. To ensure that the FL model continues to operate, SSP evolves the FL into an adaptive fuzzy system. Despite the natural drop in AUC, due to increasing drift, SSP continues to maintain high performance by rebalancing feature importance. This mirrors real-world phishing evolution, where new tactics (e.g., shorter, cleaner URLs or deceptive SSL certificates) invalidate old assumptions.

3.8 Drift Detection

SSP uses ADWIN (Adaptive Windowing) and monitors for a drop in accuracy (e.g. >5%) and triggers an update for the model's feature sets. ADWIN creates a window (data matrix) of observed feature distributions which is compared as sub-windows to the previous output. Incase, the difference between the sub-windows exceeds a statistical threshold or Statistical rigor (via Hoeffding bounds) then a drift is declared by the following steps:

W: the current adaptive window of size n
$W = W_1 \cup W_2$, split into two adjacent sub-windows:

- W_1: older part (size n_1)
- W_2: newer part (size n_2)
- $n = n_1 + n_2$

For each sub-window, define:

- $\hat{u}_1$: mean of W_1
- $\hat{u}_2$: mean of W_2

Hoeffding's inequality gives a bound on the difference between the true mean and the sample mean. For a real-valued random variable $X \in [0,1]$, with mean μ, and sample mean $\hat{u}$, the probability that $\hat{u}$ deviates from μ by more than ϵ is bounded by:

$$P(|\hat{u}-\mu| \geq \epsilon) \leq 2e^{-2n\epsilon^2} \tag{10}$$

ADWIN defines a threshold ϵ such that the probability difference is below a confidence parameter δ. ADWIN declares a **drift** when: $|\hat{u}_1 - \hat{u}_2| > \epsilon$

3.9 Update Membership Functions

After a drift is detected, SSP extracts the latest data samples for the affected feature(s) which are referred to as, 'adaptive dataset for MF recalibration'. SSP computes updated membership parameters which are fed back to the 'Pre Processing and Feature Extraction' module for fuzzification. The process then continues without human input till AUC is back within an acceptable range. A fall or rise in detection ratios are a trigger for features or weights to be auto-updated. CL's introduction in Table 2 and static features across phishing attacks ensures that Association Rule Mining (ARM) such as, Apriori or FP-Growth are applied to discover frequent item-sets and association rules. This data mining technique, discovers interesting, frequent patterns or relationships between variables in large datasets such as, "When X and Y happen together, Z is very likely to also occur". Hence, if the features of OL1, OL2, with combined with CL are true, then it is phishing. The FL selects features that appear most frequently in rules with high support, high confidence and predict phishing (core layer). Hence, a truly independent adaptive system. The sample process for a URL re-adaptation is:

x (URL length values) = {45,50,52,60,72,80,83,90,97,105}
a = 10th percentile(x) ≈ 46
b = Median(x) ≈ 76
c = 90th percentile(x) ≈ 101
SSP redefines the triangular MF for "Long URL":

$$\mu_{Long}(x) = 0 \text{ if } x \leq a \text{ or } x \geq c \text{ or } ((x-a)/(b-a)) \text{ if } a < x < b \text{ or } ((c-x)/(c-b))b < x < c \tag{11}$$

For e.g., Prior to drift detection, Long URL was defined as: MF Parameters (a, b, c) = (60, 100, 140). A URL length of 85 → $\mu_{Long}(85)$ = 0.625. Post ADWIN induced drift detection, long URL was defined as MF Parameters (a, b, c) = (46, 76, 101). The same URL length (85) → $\mu_{Long}(85) = (101-85)/(101-76) = 0.64$. Hence, phishing attackers are now using shorter URLs. Post detection of data drift the following flow occurs:

```
Extract New Data → Run ARM → Is CL valid? → Rank Feature Freq. → Select Top Features → Update Feature Set
```

Example logic:

- Rule 1: IF "SSL = invalid" AND "URL length = long" → phishing [conf: 90%]
- Rule 2: IF "keyword = login" → phishing [conf: 80%]
- Rule 3: IF "has subdomain = yes" AND "SSL = invalid" → phishing [conf: 85%]
- Hence, the most frequently occurring features are: `SSL is invalid; URL length is long; has subdomain; and keyword = login`

Post being re-routed back to become the selected features to reconfigure the FL detection engine. This is explained via the pseudocode which initializes, Feature extractor (F), Classifier or Fuzzy Inference System (FIS), ADWIN drift detector with delta = 0.05, RuleSet R = initial fuzzy rules or CBA-based association rules, FeatureWeights W = initial weights (from training or CBA), and Thresholds T = decision boundaries for phishing classification.

```
Start:
  For each incoming sample (x_i, label_i):

  # Step 1: Extract and normalize features
  features_i = Normalize(F(x_i)) # Apply Min-Max scaling
  prediction_i = FIS.predict(features_i, R, W)

  # Step 2: Measure prediction error
  error_i = ComputeError(prediction_i, label_i)
  ADWIN.update(error_i)

  # Step 3: Check for concept drift
  If ADWIN.detected_change():
    Log("Drift detected at sample", i)

  # Step 4: Re-evaluate feature importance
  NewFeatures, NewWeights = RecomputeFeature-
Set(StreamWindow)

  # Step 5: Update rules
  R = UpdateRules(NewFeatures)    # e.g., via CBA or ARM
  W = NewWeights

  # Step 6: Re-calibrate thresholds (optional)
  T = RecomputeThresholds(StreamWindow)
    Log("Rule set and weights updated")

  # Step 7: Continue with updated model
  Log("Prediction:", prediction_i)
```

4 Results

SSP's novel adaptive fuzzy logic, auto-updating feature weights, and layered inference, achieved detection accuracy comparable or higher to recent LLM-based models such as PhishLLM and KnowPhish, but at a fraction of the computational cost and with significantly lower latency. Unlike LLM-based methods, which require powerful hardware, high memory bandwidth, and API integration with multimodal reasoning agents, our FL engine can operate effectively on consumer-grade independent systems while maintaining real-time performance. Moreover, SSP's transparent decision-making process and tunable drift detection mechanism via ADWIN makes it suitable for environments where explainability, stability, and adaptability are crucial, such as, enterprise security gateways or embedded security appliances. During the course of our research, we analysed our results with and without drift and generated Fuzzy Logic (Pre-Drift) with AUC of 1.00, Fuzzy Logic (Post-Drift) with AUC of 0.984, Rule-Based (Pre-Drift) AUC of 0.981, and Rule-Based (Post-Drift) with AUC of 0.987.

FL started with a perfect score (1.0) and maintains a high AUC (0.984) after adapting to data drift. Rule-Based Detection, which was not adapted, displayed a slight performance fluctuation. Surprisingly, it improves marginally post-drift but did not learn from evolving threats. Static FL (pre-drift) models rely on frozen membership functions that no longer align with new attack patterns while adaptive (post-drift) fuzzy detection models significantly outperform static ones. Static fuzzy detections initially performed well (AUC $\approx$ 0.97 – 1.0), it typically degrades under real-world concept drift to AUCs around 0.85–0.90. Adaptive FL model maintained high detection performance over time (AUC $\approx$ 0.98) and SSP's drift trained FL models consistently sustain AUCs $\approx$ 0.98–1.00, making them suitable for real-time phishing defence. Hence, FL models that can be updated in real-time, using membership functions and adaptive weights, makes them suitable to detect phishing pages as they update their strategies.

SSP is designed to detect phishing campaigns that are advanced, undetectable, and evade counter-measure such as the ones built into all modern web browsers. This platform has been able to achieve higher detection rates as compared to web browsers owing to the use of FL and weights assigned to feature of a website. Thus, ensuring detection of phishing attacks cloaking behind splash pages, obfuscated JavaScript and forms, and URL blocking techniques such as base64 URI.

Fig. 3. Gmail Phishing URL: static.160.118.216.95.clients.your-server.de *or* IP: 95.216.118.160

Fig. 4. Gmail Phishing URL https://gmaii. email *or* IP: 52.85.49.51

Our research chose to detect phishing attacks of Gmail, Yahoo, and Proton accounts as we assumed that the browsers could easily detect and block such pages. However, that was not was results of SSP's scanning and feed generation. This section highlights two out of many samples of attacks on Gmail, Yahoo! Mail, and Proton which remained undetectable by web browsers (as of 17 July, 2025). On an average SSP [17] has detected 300 true positive phishing pages per month across the IPv4 and IPv6 spectrum of the internet with an average precision rate of 98.4 and recall rate of 99.7.

Gmail Phishing Pages: In Fig. 3, the website escaped heuristic scanners since the page uses text that is different from the current Gmail page. Figure 4 site replaces the icon main icon (in the centre of the page) with Google Gemini which presumably confused the browser's security engine and passes this as a valid URL. Yahoo! Mail Phishing Pages in Figs. 5 and 6 along with Proton Mail Phishing Pages in Figs. 7 and 8 were undetected as they did not have text that was suspicious to the inbuilt web browser's

Fig. 5. Yahoo Mail! Phishing URL: sv24-panel.tsfast24.top *or* IP: 213.142.133.228:10204

Fig. 6. Yahoo Mail! Phishing URL: nmailweb-svc.onrender.com *or* IP: 216.24.57.252

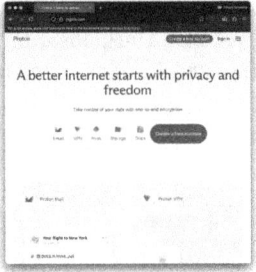

Fig. 7. Proton Mail Phishing URL: jngxin.com *or* vmi2216411.contaboserver.net *or* 109.199.119.131.sslip.io *or* vmi2216411.contaboserver.net *or* IP: 109.199.119.131

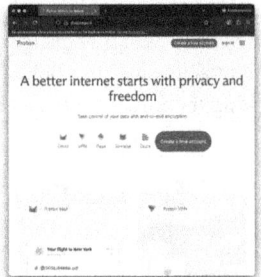

Fig. 8. Proton Mail Phishing URL: dotcompc.ir *or* static.201.254.107.91.clients.your-server.de *or* static.201.254.107.91.clients.your-server.de *or* 91.107.254.201.sslip.io,*or* IP: 91.107.254.201

heuristic scanner or were not listed in blacklists. As the browsers do not publish YARA or blacklists we assume that Proton and Yahoo! phishing pages were undetected as they are new sites. However, SSP detected and included the sites in its feed.

The FL algorithm was also able to detect a novel phishing attack. This attack commences when an attacker sends a link to a target which prompts them click on Proton sign-in link. This would automatically redirect the user to a valid Proton Mail webpage that would ask them to 'authorise' the action. This valid popup, if accepted, would grant access of the target's logged-in Proton account's inbox to the attacker's Proton account. At this point, the attacker would have complete access to all data in a Proton account. This was uncovered at: adam.dovah.ir, with DNS: 172.245.156.13.sslip.io, and 193.188.21.171.sslip.io, and static.176.118.88.23.clients.your-server.de. This finding has been included in this paper as further proof that our research is able to detect novel phishing attacks by auto-adapting.

5 Conclusion

Any model that does not adapt to a changing threat landscape, via feature updates, risks failure and a decrease in their relevance. This underscores the importance of data-driven feature tuning in maintaining detection efficacy in evolving threat landscapes.

Table 4. Phishing Detection Model Comparison

System	Detection Accuracy (%)	Inference Time (ms)	Hardware	Throughput
SSP	98.0	~50	CPU (Edge)	~1 s per page
PhishLLM	97.8	~4000	GPU / Cloud	~0.1 s per page
KnowPhish	96.5	~3000	GPU / Cloud	>10 s/webpage
PhishAgent	98.2	~3500	GPU / Cloud	~1–5 ms/query
Qwen2.5–1.5B (Small LLM)	97.6	~250	CPU/GPU	107K–2.2M sites/$100

In Table 4, SSP offers exceptional cost-efficiency, high transparency, and near-LLM performance while, LLMs offer better performance on semantic, adversarial, or visual edge cases but at high computational cost. Small LLMs like Qwen2.5 offer a middle ground, useful for hybrid deployments with fuzzy systems. Fuzzy Logic in Table 5 performs competitively (96% accuracy) with low overhead and high explainability while, PhishLLM offers the highest performance, particularly in complex edge cases.

Table 5. Benchmark Comparison: UCI Phishing Dataset

Model	Accuracy (%)	Precision	Recall	F1-Score	AUC
Fuzzy Logic Engine (SSP)	96.0	0.98	0.99	0.98	0.98
CNN	94.3	0.94	0.92	0.93	0.96
Transformer	96.8	0.96	0.97	0.96	0.98
PhishLLM	97.8	0.98	0.98	0.98	0.99
Qwen2.5–1.5B	97.6	0.97	0.97	0.97	0.98

LLMs demonstrate superior performance in handling obfuscated, multilingual, and visually deceptive phishing attacks through multimodal reasoning, SSP offers a compelling tradeoff by presenting an interpretable, cost-efficient, and easily deployable platform. SSP has achieved Homoglyph detection since it detects domains based on Levenstein distance. However, a comparison (Table 6) of the International Domain Names (IDN) detection has scope of improvement. Future work will focus on integrating lightweight LLM capabilities into SSP to handle IDN edge case, thereby creating a hybrid detection framework that combines semantic depth with algorithmic efficiency.

Table 6. International Domain Names (IDN) Comparison of FL and LLMs

Model	Strengths	Limitations
Fuzzy Logic	IDN: Flags non-ASCII characters or domain encodings like xn--,	IDN: Cannot parse semantic meaning at the language level
LLM-Based	IDN: Learns token-level irregularities in domain names, including use of encoded or transliterated tokens	IDN: Requires pretraining. Needs exposure to IDN obfuscation patterns during fine-tuning

Disclosure of Interests. The authors have no competing interests to declare that are relevant to the content of this article.

References

1. Hossain, E., Khan, I., Un-Noor, F., Sikander, S.S., Sunny, M.S.H.: Application of big data and machine learning in smart grid, and associated security concerns: a review. IEEE Access. 7, 13960–13988 (2019). https://doi.org/10.1109/ACCESS.2019.2894819
2. Sikder, A.K., Petracca, G., Aksu, H., Jaeger, T., Uluagac, A.S.: A survey on sensor-based threats to internet-of-things (IoT) devices and applications. arXiv:20181802.02041
3. Sun, H., Xu, M., Zhao, P.: Modeling malicious hacking data breach risks. N. Am. Actuar. J. 1–19 (2020). https://doi.org/10.1080/10920277.2020.1752255
4. IBM: What is social engineering? IBM (2022). https://www.ibm.com/think/topics/social-engineering#:~:text=According%20to%20the%20IBM%20X,the%20most%20costly%20data%20breaches
5. Sjouwerman, S.: 91% of cyberattacks begin with spear phishing email. KnowBe4 (2012). https://blog.knowbe4.com/bid/252429/91-of-cyberattacks-begin-with-spear-phishing-email
6. Sjouwerman, S.: New threat report finds nearly 90% of cyber threats involve social engineering. KnowBe4 (2024). https://blog.knowbe4.com/nearly-90-of-threats-involve-social-enginering
7. Valimail: Valimail report reveals 3 billion spoofed emails are sent every day. Valimail (2021). https://valimail.com/newsroom/valimail-report-reveals-3-billion-spoofed-emails-are-sent-every-day/
8. Federal Bureau of Investigation. 2023 Internet crime report (2024). https://www.ic3.gov/annualreport/reports/2023_ic3report.pdf
9. CECOM CIO G6 Cybersecurity. Secure our world — CECOM raises awareness about phishing. U.S. Army (2024). https://army.mil/article/280696/secure_our_world_cecom_raises_awareness_about_phishing
10. CurrentWare: What is the best email provider? Top free & paid email services in 2025 (2023). https://www.currentware.com/blog/best-email-service-providers/#:~:text=for%20business%20users.-,Gmail,and%20customizability%20to%20its%20users
11. Hosch, W. L., The Editors of Encyclopedia Britannica: Chrome. Encyclopedia Britannica (2025). https://www.britannica.com/technology/Chrome
12. Aburrous, M., Hossain, M.A., Thabatah, F., Dahal, K.: Intelligent phishing website detection system using fuzzy techniques. In: 2008 3rd International Conference on Information and Communication Technologies: From Theory to Applications, Damascus, Syria, pp. 1–6 (2008). https://doi.org/10.1109/ICTTA.2008.4530019

13. Liu, R., Lu, X., Zhang, H., Liu, C., Zhang, M.: PhishLLM: accurate and stealthy phishing detection via large language models. In Proceedings of the 33rd USENIX Security Symposium (USENIX Security 24). USENIX Association (2024). https://www.usenix.org/conference/usenixsecurity24/presentation/liu-ruofan
14. Li, Y., Duan, H., Wang, Y.: KnowPhish: a knowledge-enhanced framework for phishing webpage detection. arXiv:2403.02253 (2024)
15. Sun, Y., Gao, C., Shen, S., Zhu, S.: PhishAgent: skill-agent-based multimodal framework for phishing website detection. arXiv:2408.10738 (2024)
16. Chen, M., Hu, K., Liu, J., Zhang, Q.: Improving phishing email detection via small LLMs: an empirical study of Qwen2.5–1.5B. arXiv:2505.00034 (2025)
17. Srivastava, A.: ServerSecurityProject (SSP): Open-source passive Internet scanner for phishing and credential harvesting pages [Computer software]. GitHub (n.d.). https://github.com/AadyaSrivastava/ServerSecurityProject

Intelligent Analytics from Wearable Flexible Sensors for Next-Generation Health Diagnostics

Xufu Xiang[1,2(✉)], Weifang Li[1], Xiaotao Lin[1], Gang Wang[1], and Chungen Qian[1,2(✉)]

[1] Department of Reagent Research and Development, Shenzhen YHLO Biotech Co., Ltd., Shenzhen, Guangdong, China
xiangxufu@hust.edu.cn, gen.qian@szyhlo.com

[2] The Key Laboratory for Biomedical Photonics of MOE at Wuhan National Laboratory for Optoelectronics-Hubei Bioinformatics and Molecular Imaging Key Laboratory, Systems Biology Theme, Department of Biomedical Engineering, College of Life Science and Technology, Huazhong University of Science and Technology, Wuhan 430074, China

Abstract. Advances in Internet of Things (IoT) technology drive demand for affordable, compact, lightweight, and flexible wearable devices. Flexible devices integrate functional materials (e.g., nanoparticles, nanowires, carbon nanotubes, conductive polymers) with flexible substrates (e.g., fiber fabrics, polymers), combining substrate flexibility with material properties like conductivity, photothermal response, and strength. Encompassing electronic (e.g., flexible displays, circuits) and non-electronic types (e.g., paper-based chips, actuators), they find applications in energy storage, biomimetics, biomedicine, and beyond. This review covers the constituent materials, functional material patterning methods, and biomedical applications of flexible devices, focusing on sensing/monitoring, disease treatment/healthcare, and artificial organs.

Keywords: flexible devices · flexible substrates · functional materials · patterning · biomedical applications

1 Introduction

Silicon-based semiconductors, dominant in the 1960s due to abundance, low cost, and robustness, propelled early electronics but yielded rigid circuits incompatible with modern wearable flexibility requirements. Concurrently, thinning silicon to 100–200 μm enabled flexible solar cells on substrates for space applications [1]. A breakthrough came in the 1970s with Shirakawa's synthesis of highly conductive polyacetylene, ushering in π-conjugated organic electronics [2]. Conductive polymers and organic semiconductors, compatible with large-area, low-cost printing on flexible substrates, offered plastic-like flexibility, partially meeting demands for flexible electronics, as demonstrated by Heeger's flexible PAn/PET OLEDs in 1992[3].

Beyond organics, integrating inorganic materials (superior in electrical/thermal conductivity but inherently inflexible) onto flexible substrates is another major fabrication

---

X. Xiang and W. Li—These authors contributed equally

route. Structural design innovations impart flexibility, such as Rogers' transfer of semiconductor nanoribbons to pre-stretched PDMS or assembly of rigid silicon units on flexible substrates [4]. Recent research focuses on inorganic conductors (metal nanoparticles, nanowires, liquid metals, graphene, CNTs, MXene) for flexible electrodes fabricated via techniques like printing, coating, and self-assembly [5].

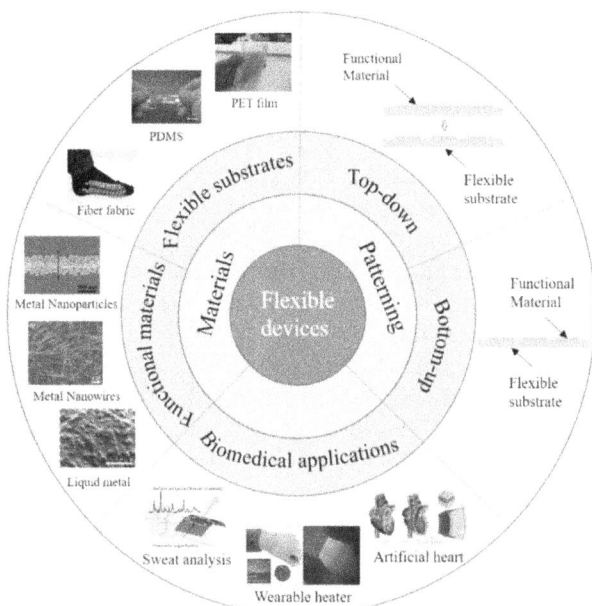

Fig. 1. Overview of flexible device materials, patterning, and biomedical applications.

Flexible electronics finds broad application in displays, energy storage, circuits, and notably, sensors. Significant research targets flexible sensors due to their potential in healthcare, human-computer interfaces, and robotics. The 21st century saw rapid growth in wearable health monitors. Products include MC10's BioStamp nPoint biosensing patch (posture, activity, sleep, EMG), Xenoma's temperature-monitoring smart sleepwear linked to HVAC, and Hexoskin's vital-sign-tracking smart shirts [8]. Flexible consumer electronics advanced with foldable smartphones from Royole, Huawei, Samsung, and Motorola since 2018.

Flexible sensors are diverse. By application, they include pressure, environmental (gas, temperature, humidity), strain, magnetoimpedance, and heat flow sensors. By mechanism, common types are resistive, capacitive, piezoelectric, and piezomagnetic. Despite variations, core components typically comprise sensitive materials, flexible substrates, electrodes, and insulating encapsulation.

This review focuses on three key aspects for biomedical flexible devices (Fig. 1): (1) Flexible substrates (PET, PDMS, PVA, PEN, PI, fabrics) [6–14] and functional materials (metal nanoparticles, nanowires, liquid metals, graphene, CNTs, conductive polymers); (2) Patterning methods for functional material integration; (3) Biomedical applications: sensing/monitoring, disease treatment/healthcare, and artificial organs. Practical challenges are also discussed.

2 Materials for Fabricating Flexible Devices

2.1 Flexible Substrates

Flexible substrates provide essential mechanical support and govern the deformation behavior of flexible devices, characterized by inherent lightweight, thin, and pliable properties. Specific application requirements dictate critical material properties, including tailored mechanical strength, optical characteristics, corrosion resistance, and biocompatibility; for instance, flexible electronics necessitate substrates with high electrical insulation to mitigate leakage currents. Practical viability further demands substrates to be cost-effective, accessible, and durable. Polymers constitute the predominant class of flexible substrates, with common materials including PET film, PDMS, PI, PEN, PVA, and fiber fabric. PET, PI, and PEN exhibit low elongation and high thermal stability, rendering them ideal for flexible displays [6–8, 15–17]. PDMS features a low Young's modulus, high transparency, corrosion resistance, and biocompatibility, making it suitable for skin-conformable wearable biosensors. Fiber fabrics offer breathability and comfort for long-term wearable medical applications. Additionally, cellulose serves as a substrate for flexible paper-based electronics due to its biodegradability and low environmental impact.

2.2 Functional Materials

Functional materials are essential for imparting specific capabilities to flexible devices. Key categories include: nanoparticles [9], nanowires [10], and liquid metals [11], as well as graphene [18], carbon nanotubes [19], conductive polymers [20], and MXene [21].

1). Organic Semiconductors: Offer inherent flexibility, overcoming silicon's rigidity. Compatible with low-cost, large-area solution processing (e.g., printing) on flexible substrates.
2). Metallic Materials: Provide superior electrical conductivity. Thin foils (e.g., Cu, Sn) offer bendability. Nanoparticles, nanowires, or liquid metals (e.g., EGaIn alloys) dispersed in solvents enable coating/printing onto flexible substrates, enhancing flexibility, stretchability, and transparency. Microfluidic/screen printing enables patterned circuits.
3). Carbon-Based Materials (Graphene, CNTs): Exhibit excellent electrical/thermal conductivity, chemical stability, low toxicity, and high surface area. Easily functionalized for flexible sensors (electromechanical, temperature, humidity, electrochemical) and electrodes monitoring physiology/disease markers [22].

4). Conductive Polymers: Include intrinsic types (e.g., PAn, PPy, PEDOT - conductivity via π-electron conjugation) and composites (conductive fillers in polymer matrices). PEDOT:PSS, offering high conductivity, thermal stability, and solution processability, is widely used in flexible pressure, stress, and touch sensors.
5). MXenes: 2D transition metal carbides/nitrides (surface -OH/-O groups). Possess excellent conductivity, hydrophilicity, and dispersion stability, making them ideal printable inks for energy storage, biomedicine, and actuators.

Stimuli-Responsive Materials: Exploit non-electrical properties. Cellulose's hydrophilicity enables paper-based microfluidics. Hydrogels, shape-memory polymers, liquid crystal polymers, electroactive polymers, and magnetic materials respond to chemical, thermal, optical, electrical, or magnetic stimuli, enabling flexible actuators for biomimetic drives, soft robotics, and artificial muscles.

3 Methods for Fabricating Flexible Devices Functi

3.1 Methods for Fabricating Paper-Based Microfluidic Devices

Introduced by Whitesides in 2007, microfluidic paper-based analytical devices (μPADs) utilize cellulose capillary action to direct fluid flow, offering advantages over conventional glass/PDMS chips including low cost, simplicity, biodegradability, and pump-free operation. Consequently, μPADs find broad application in environmental monitoring, food safety, and medical diagnostics. Fabrication methods, summarized in Fig. 2, comprise seven primary categories:

1). Drawing/Embossing: Hydrophobic barriers (e.g., wax, PDMS) are drawn/plotted (Figs. 2a,b, 3c) or stamped onto paper.
2). Cutting: Physical patterning via programmable knife cutting (Figs. 2c, 3e) or precise laser ablation (Figs. 2d, 3l).
3). Direct Printing: High-throughput patterning using wax printing with heating (Figs. 2e, 3d) or roll-to-roll flexographic printing of hydrophobic polymers (e.g., polystyrene) (Figs. 2f, 3f).
4). Heat-Transfer: Patterned hydrophobic materials (e.g., alkylating agents, paraffin, hot-melt adhesive) are transferred from carriers to paper via co-heating (Figs. 2g, h, 3j, m, p).
5). Mask-Wax Penetration: Wax penetrates unmasked paper regions via dipping or screen printing (Figs. 2i, j, 3g, i).
6). Lithography: Original SU-8 photolithography defines patterns via UV exposure and development (Figs. 2k, 3a). Water-soluble PUA photolithography offers an alternative (Figs. 2l, 3o).
7). Hydrophobic-Selective Hydrophilic Modification: Paper undergoes global hydrophobic treatment (e.g., alkyl ketene dimer, polystyrene, OTS, TMOS) followed by localized hydrophilic patterning via plasma treatment, inkjet etching, UV/O_3 exposure, or surfactant/NaOH penetration using masks (Figs. 2m-o, 3b,k).

Additional methods include laser-induced hydrophilicity on pre-treated papers, stamp-controlled wax patterning, cavity carving, and high-resolution (10–20 μm) bottom-up assembly of cellulose microfibers.

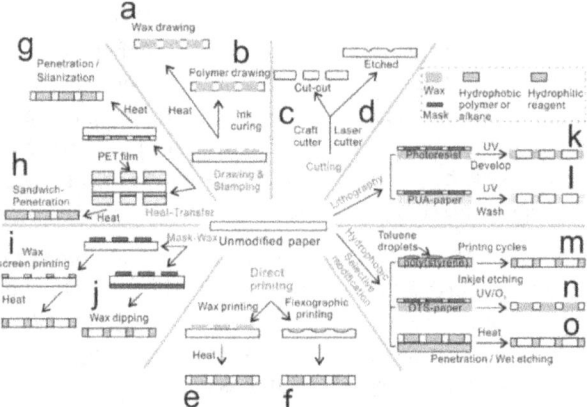

Fig. 2. μPAD fabrication methods: (a) Wax drawing/embossing, (b) Polymer patterning, (c) Knife cutting, (d) Laser cutting, (e) Wax jet printing, (f) Flexographic printing, (g) Hydrophobic layer/silanization, (h) Sandwich infiltration, (i) Wax screen printing, (j) Mask-wax dip, (k) SU-8 lithography, (l) PUA lithography, (m) Ink etching, (n) UV/O_3 plasma, (o) Surfactant etching.

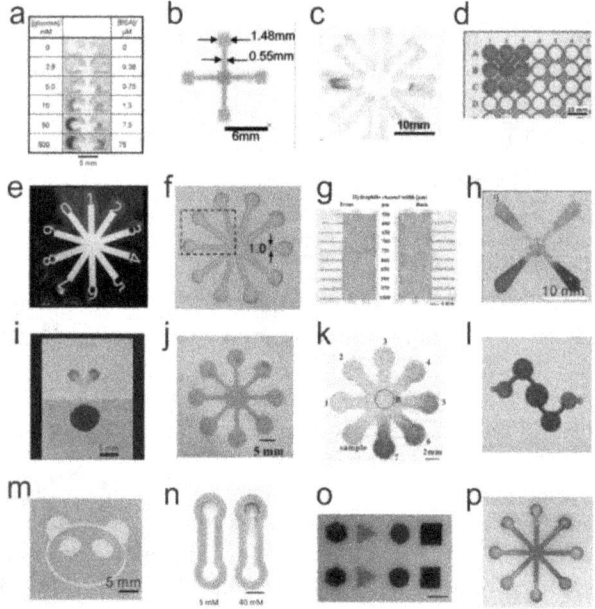

Fig. 3. Fabricated μPADs: (a) SU-8 lithography, (b) inkjet etching, (c) PDMS hand-painted, (d) wax printing, (e) programmed tool cutting, (f) flexographic printing, (g) wax screen-printing, (h) laser modification, (i) Mask-Wax dipping, (j) paper mask alkylation, (k) OTS/UV-O_3, (l) laser cutting, (m) paraffin thermal permeation, (n) micro-bumps/wax, (o) PUA lithography, (p) laser-cut/hot-melt lamination.

3.2 Methods for Fabricating Flexible Electronic Devices

3.2.1 Flexible Electronic Circuits Assembled by Metal Nanoparticles

Solution evaporation-driven nanoparticle self-assembly offers a simple, effective route for constructing well-defined optoelectronic and electronic structures. Key demonstrations include utilizing the coffee-ring effect in inkjet printing to assemble flexible transparent circuits (Magdassi et al.) and AgNPs into micron-scale lines on glass (Song et al.). Song et al. further exploited liquid-bridge effects to fabricate submicron AgNP circuits on PDMS (Fig. 4a) and silicon-templated wavy circuits for flexible sensing. Minari et al. directed AuNP assembly into micron circuits via vacuum ultraviolet-patterned hydrophilic regions on hydrophobic substrates (Fig. 4b). Liu's team employed PDMS-confined coffee rings for high-throughput 2D pattern assembly, transferred to PDMS as transparent stretchable electrodes (Fig. 4c. Nanoparticle deposition on wettability-patterned paper substrates also enables paper-based flexible electronics.

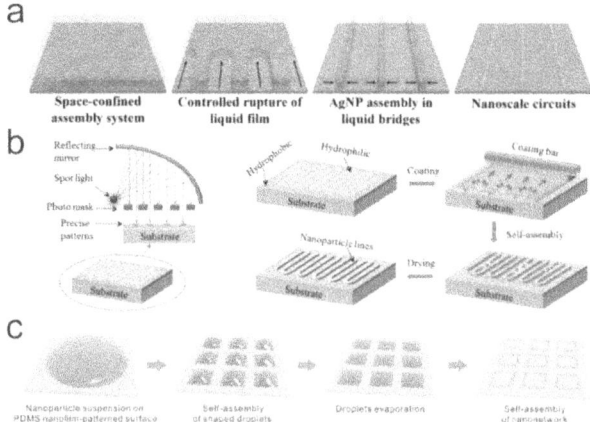

Fig. 4. Nanoparticle-assembled circuits: (a) AgNPs liquid bridge [9], (b) AuNPs UV-etching [48], (c) PDMS coffee ring [49].

3.2.2 Silver Nanowire (AgNW) Patterning for Flexible Transparent Electrodes

AgNWs are preferred for flexible transparent electrodes due to their conductivity, ductility, and optical transparency. Patterning is essential to enhance performance and electrical isolation. Methods are broadly categorized:

1). Verall Coating-Selective Removal/Transfer: Involves coating AgNWs uniformly followed by selective ablation (laser, etching (lithography, micro-contact printing), or microchannel filling/transfer. Plasma welding also enables patterning. These top-down approaches incur material waste from removal.
2). Ask-Based Patterning: Utilizes physical masks (wax, photolithographic Perelin PVC, PDMS) deposited via filtration, spraying, or spin coating. Mask removal reveals the pattern, but material waste on masks and potential resolution loss are drawbacks.
3). Elective Coating: Minimizes waste by direct deposition. Techniques include screen printing (50 μm resolution), direct writing, inkjet printing groove printing, and

capillary confinement. Self-assembly (pre-stretched substrates, standing waves, ice-templating) offers novel routes but struggles with arbitrary patterning. Wettability-assisted patterning confines AgNWs to hydrophilic regions via spin/drip coating on plasma-treated or laser-patterned templates, enabling high-resolution (8 μm), transferable electrodes (Figs. 5 and 6).

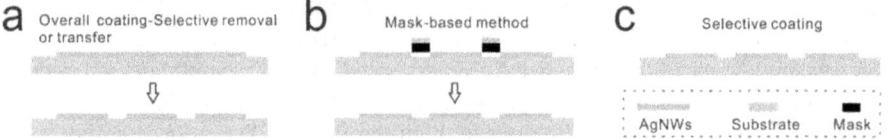

Fig. 5. A figure caption is always placed below the illustration. Short captions are centered, while long ones are justified. The macro button chooses the correct format automatically.

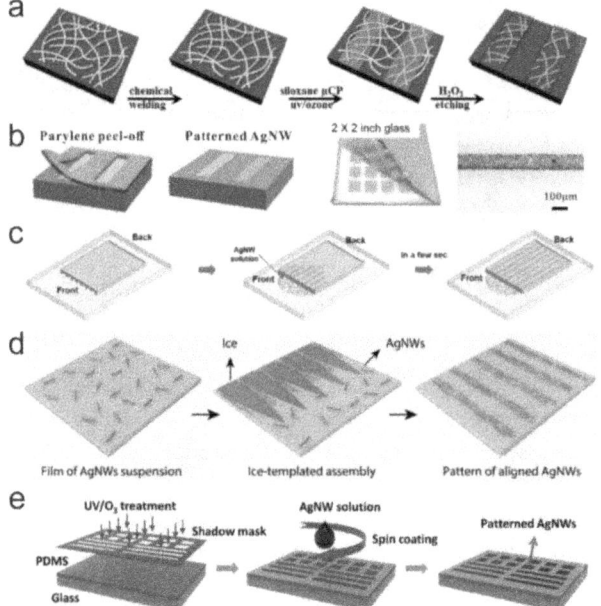

Fig. 6. AgNW Patterning: (a) Microcontact, (b) Parylene mask-spray, (c) Capillary force, (d) Ice template, (e) Wettability-patterned PDMS.

4 Biomedical Applications of Flexible Devices

4.1 Biomedical Sensing and Monitoring

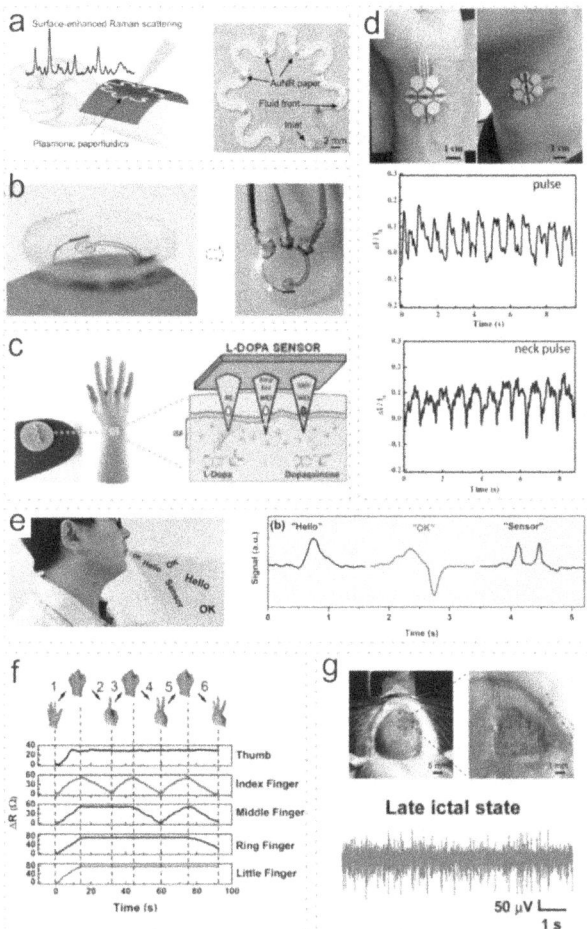

Fig. 7. Flexible Biomedical Sensors: (a) Biofluid-sweat, (b) Biofluid-tear, (c) Microneedle-sensing, (d) Pulse-monitoring, (e) Motion-speech, (f) Motion-finger, (g) In vivo-recording.

Flexible wearable sensors enable critical monitoring of physiological indicators (blood pressure, glucose, ECG, activity) and biomarkers in biofluids (sweat, tears, interstitial fluid) for disease management. Paper-based microfluidic devices facilitate continuous sweat analysis (Fig. 7a), while electrochemical sensors quantify tear glucose via contact lenses (Fig. 7b). Functionalized graphene enables wireless bacterial detection on enamel, and microneedle sensors permit transdermal drug monitoring in interstitial fluid (Fig. 7c). Motion recognition employs self-powered e-skins (rGO/PVDF) for multi-modal sensing and pulse detection (Fig. 7d), polyaniline membranes for speech analysis

(Fig. 7e), and liquid metal strain sensors for joint motion tracking (Fig. 7f). Implantable applications include PDMS-liquid metal electrodes for neural signal recording (Fig. 7g). Commercial implementations encompass health bracelets, smart textiles, and flexible oximeters (Fig. 8).

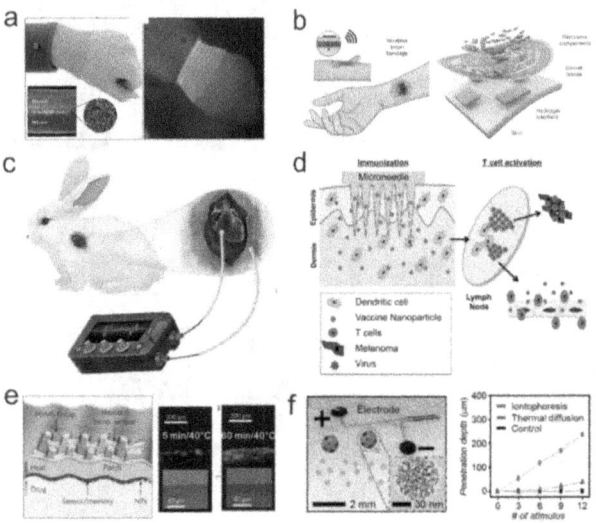

Fig. 8. Flexible Therapeutics: (a) Thermotherapy-heaters, (b) Smart-dressings, (c) Cardiac-correction, (d) Microneedle-delivery, (e) Thermo-release, (f) Electro-penetration.

4.2 Artificial Organs

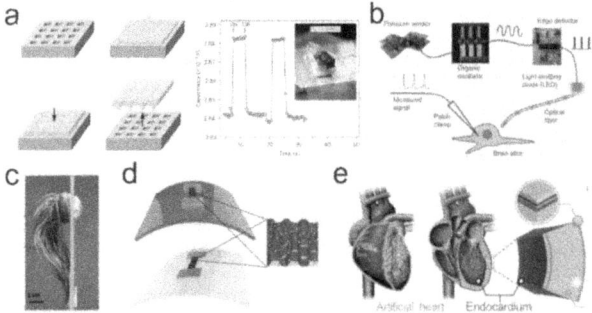

Fig. 9. Flexible Bionic Organs: (a) E-skin–neural interface, (b) Neuro-bidirectional, (c) Vision-bionic, (d) Olfactory-sensing, (e) Cardiac-blood pump.

Artificial organs (skin, eyes, limbs) exemplify flexible devices' biomedical potential. Research focuses on emulating sensory perception: Bao's team developed e-skin using micropyramid-structured PDMS dielectrics in FETs, detecting subtle stimuli like fly contact (Fig. 9a), and created mechanoreceptors translating pressure to digital signals that stimulate neurons (Fig. 9b). Additional advances include bionic electrochemical eyes (Fig. 9c), turbinate-mimetic noses for hydrogen sensing (Fig. 9d), and artificial hearts (Fig. 9e), progressively realizing science-fiction concepts through flexible electronics.

5 Conclusions

Flexible devices integrate functional materials (organic/inorganic electronics) with compliant substrates (paper, textiles, PET, PDMS), forming inherently thin, portable, and wearable systems. These bendable/stretchable platforms enable applications across biomedicine, displays, energy storage, and circuits. This review summarizes advances in substrate materials, functional components, patterning methodologies, and biomedical implementations of both electronic and non-electronic (e.g., paper-based) variants.

Despite progress, key challenges persist: long-term reliability under environmental degradation (oxidation, UV exposure, mechanical fatigue) necessitates enhanced material stability and manufacturing processes. Scalable production requires cost-effective solution-processing/printing technologies like 2D inks. Future development demands interdisciplinary convergence of nano-materials, micro-fabrication, flexible substrates, electrochemistry, wireless systems, and AI to realize intelligent wearable devices for real-time health monitoring and treatment.

Acknowledgments. I sincerely thank Dr. Peng Ma for her expert guidance and acknowledge the technical support provided by the Microfluidic Laboratory of HUST.

Disclosure of Interests. The authors declare that they have no competing interests.

References

1. Ray, K.A.: Flexible solar cell arrays for increased space power. IEEE T Aero Elec Sys. **1**, 107–115 (1967)
2. Shirakawa, H., Louis, E.J., MacDiarmid, A.G., Chiang, C.K., Heeger, A.J.: Synthesis of electrically conducting organic polymers: halogen derivatives of polyacetylene, (CH)x. J. Chem. Soc. Chem. Commun. **16**, 578–580 (1977)
3. Gustafsson, G., Cao, Y., Treacy, G.M., Klavetter, F., Colaneri, N., Heeger, A.J.: Flexible light-emitting diodes made from soluble conducting polymers. Nature **357**(6378), 477–479 (1992)
4. Sun, Y.G., Choi, W.M., Jiang, H.Q., Huang, Y.G.Y., Rogers, J.A.: Controlled buckling of semiconductor nanoribbons for stretchable electronics. Nat. Nanotechnol. **1**(3), 201–207 (2006)
5. Kim, D.H., Ahn, J.H., Choi, W.M., Kim, H.S., Kim, T.H., Song, J.Z., et al.: Stretchable and foldable silicon integrated circuits. Science **320**(5875), 507–511 (2008)
6. Hu, L.B., Kim, H.S., Lee, J.Y., Peumans, P., Cui, Y.: Scalable coating and properties of transparent, flexible, silver nanowire electrodes. ACS Nano **4**(5), 2955–2963 (2010)
7. Han, J.K., Yang, J.K., Gao, W.W., Bai, H.: Ice-templated, large-area silver nanowire pattern for flexible transparent electrode. Adv. Funct. Mater. **31**(16), 2010155 (2021)
8. Jeerapan, I., Sempionatto, J.R., Pavinatto, A., You, J.M., Wang, J.: Stretchable biofuel cells as wearable textile-based self-powered sensors. J Mater Chem A. **4**(47), 18342–18353 (2016)

9. Chen, S.R., Su, M., Zhang, C., Gao, M., Bao, B., Yang, Q., et al.: Fabrication of nanoscale circuits on inkjet-printing patterned substrates. Adv. Mater. **27**(26), 3928–3933 (2015)
10. Liang, C., Su, W.M., Sun, X.Y., Hu, Y.W., Duan, J.A.: Femtosecond laser patterning wettability-assisted PDMS for fabrication of flexible silver nanowires electrodes. Adv. Mater. Interfaces **8**(19), 2100608 (2021)
11. Ma, B., Xu, C.T., Chi, J.J., Chen, J., Zhao, C., Liu, H.: A versatile approach for direct patterning of liquid metal using magnetic field. Adv. Funct. Mater. **29**(28), 1901370 (2019)
12. Mogera, U., Guo, H., Namkoong, M., Rahman, M.S., Nguyen, T., Tian, L.M.: Wearable plasmonic paper-based microfluidics for continuous sweat analysis. Sci. Adv. **8**(12), 1736 (2022)
13. Choi, S., Park, J., Hyun, W., Kim, J., Kim, J., Lee, Y.B., et al.: Stretchable heater using ligand-exchanged silver nanowire nanocomposite for wearable articular thermotherapy. ACS Nano **9**(6), 6626–6633 (2015)
14. Wu, W.J., Zhang, S.K., Wu, Z.P., Qin, S.C., Li, F.Z., Song, T.F., et al.: On the understanding of dielectric elastomer and its application for all-soft artificial heart. Sci. Bull. **66**(10), 981–990 (2021)
15. Xu, J.Y., Guo, H.D., Ding, H.Y., Wang, Q., Tang, Z.Q., Li, Z.J., et al.: Printable and recyclable conductive ink based on a liquid metal with excellent surface wettability for flexible electronics. ACS Appl. Mater. Interfaces **13**(6), 7443–7452 (2021)
16. Lamanna, L., Rizzi, F., Guido, F., Algieri, L., Marras, S., Mastronardi, V.M., et al.: Flexible and transparent aluminum-nitride-based surface-acoustic-wave device on polymeric polyethylene naphthalate. Adv. Electron. Mater. **5**(6), 1900095 (2019)
17. Mamleyev, E.R., Heissler, S., Nefedov, A., Weidler, P.G., Nordin, N., Kudryashov, V.V., et al.: Laser-induced hierarchical carbon patterns on polyimide substrates for flexible urea sensors. NPJ Flex Electron. **3**(1), 2 (2019)
18. Geim, A.K.: Graphene: status and prospects. Science **324**(5934), 1530–1534 (2009)
19. Li, J., Hu, L., Wang, L., Zhou, Y., Gruner, G., Marks, T.J.: Organic light-emitting diodes having carbon nanotube anodes. Nano Lett. **6**(11), 2472–2477 (2006)
20. Vosgueritchian, M., Lipomi, D.J., Bao, Z.A.: Highly conductive and transparent PEDOT: PSS films with a fluorosurfactant for stretchable and flexible transparent electrodes. Adv. Funct. Mater. **22**(2), 421–428 (2012)
21. Zhang, Y.Z., Wang, Y., Jiang, Q., El-Demellawi, J.K., Kim, H., Alshareef, H.N.: Mxene printing and patterned coating for device applications. Adv. Mater. **32**(21), 1908486 (2020)
22. Wang, H.M., Li, S., Lu, H.J., Zhu, M.J., Liang, H.R., Wu, X.E., et al.: Carbon-based flexible devices for comprehensive health monitoring. Small Methods **7**(2), 2201340 (2023)

Research and Implementation of Power Line Fault Diagnosis Technology Based on Wavelet Transform

Mingfeng Shi[✉], Yuke Zhao, Feifei Liu, Baolei Jia, Gaowu Huang, and Jie Shui

China Gridcom Co., Ltd., Shenzhen 518109, China
shimingfeng@sgchip.sgcc.com.cn

Abstract. To address the problems of difficult pre-judgment of power line faults, unrecognized faults, and difficult post-fault location, a power line fault diagnosis scheme based on wavelet transform is proposed. The fault types of 10 kV power line and their impact on the power grid are analyzed. The fault location algorithm was studied, and the power line fault diagnosis process and online monitoring device were designed. The validity and feasibility of the proposed method were verified using a real model. This method can effectively solve the problem of power line fault diagnosis and location in distribution networks. The large-scale application of the developed online monitoring device can significantly improve the safety and stability of distribution networks.

Keywords: 10 kV Power Line · Fault Diagnosis · Fault Location · Online Monitoring Device · Wavelet Transform

1 Introduction

With the continuous advancement of the construction of new power systems, the operation of power lines has gradually changed from passive fault handling to active defect prediction. The active defect prediction system will warn and investigate some 'gradual' faults in the distribution network before the fault occurs, such as the near-line fault of trees in the distribution line. Passive fault handling involves checking the cause of the fault and restoring the power supply after the fault occurs. The active defect early warning system is designed to detect defects at a certain distance from the distribution line during tree growth. At this time, it is insufficient to form a fault. At this stage, early warning and defect detection are performed to avoid the occurrence of faults [1–3].

The research on online monitoring of 10 kV distribution networks has always been a hot topic in the industry. Most of these studies focused on line selection and ranging, and less research has been conducted on fault identification. With the continuous improvement in the importance of distribution networks, research on power line fault identification has also increased. With the technical improvement of relay protection algorithms and devices, researchers have applied mathematics and sampling techniques to the fault identification and classification of distribution lines, which has effectively promoted the fault diagnosis of distribution network power systems. Based on traveling wave ranging and positioning, the key is to effectively collect traveling wave ranging signals, which can realize pre-fault warning, fault identification and post-fault positioning, and the current positioning accuracy is more than 150 m.

2 Common Faults of 10 kV Power Lines

There are four main types of common faults in the 10 kV power lines: single-phase grounding fault, double-phase short circuit fault, double-phase short circuit grounding fault, and three-phase short circuit fault [4]. Figure 1 (1)–(4) show simple diagrams of the four types of faults.

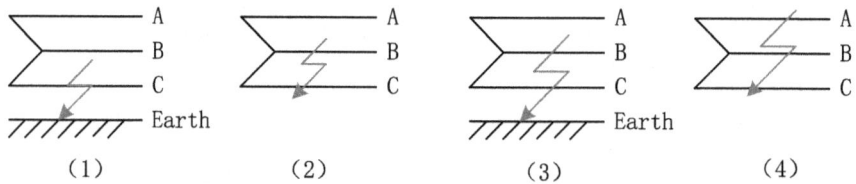

Fig. 1. Common fault types of 10 kV power lines.

2.1 Single-Phase Grounding Fault

A single-phase grounding fault refers to the connection of a single-phase power line to the earth owing to environmental factors or line insulation problems. Most of them occur during windy and thunderstorm weather. It is the main fault type in distribution networks, and its proportion is more than 80% in all faults [5].

After a single-phase ground fault occurs in the power line, the symmetry of the three-phase of the power grid is abnormal, and the three-phase neutral point will shifts, resulting in a change in the three-phase ground voltage. For example, when a single-phase ground fault occurs in phase A, the voltage and the ground capacitance current become 0, and the ground voltage and the ground capacitance current of non-fault phase B and C become $\sqrt{3}$ times the original. The analysis of the fault line shows that the amplitude of the zero-sequence current is equal to the sum of the zero-sequence current of the non-fault line when a single-phase grounding fault occurs, and the zero-sequence voltage is generated simultaneously. If the fault is not eliminated in time, long-term operation may cause the line insulation to break down, resulting in new short circuit faults.

2.2 Double-Phase Short Circuit Fault

A double-phase short circuit grounding fault refers to the short circuit phenomenon of any double-phase power line in a 10 kV distribution network owing to environmental factors or line insulation problems. It is mostly caused by factors such as aging or damage to electrical equipment and devices.

2.3 Double-Phase Short Circuit Grounding Fault

A double-phase short circuit fault refers to the short circuit phenomenon caused by the single-phase grounding of any two phases in the neutral-point-ungrounded system, which is mostly caused by lightning strike, external force damage, and other factors.

2.4 Three-Phase Short Circuit Fault

A three-phase short circuit fault refers to the short circuit of three phases in a 10 kV distribution network at the same position. This situation is relatively rare but very destructive. It is mostly caused by human factors, such as closing with a ground knife.

3 Fault Location Algorithm

The fault location algorithms of 10 kV distribution networks mainly include the single-terminal method, double-terminal method, three-terminal method, and multi-terminal method [6]. This study mainly discusses the first three algorithms.

3.1 Single-Terminal Method

The single-terminal method uses data measured at one end of the power line for ranging. The method is illustrated in Fig. 2. F represents the fault point of the power line.

$$d = \frac{1}{2} v_1 \Delta t \tag{1}$$

$$d = \frac{v_1 v_0 (t_{M0} - t_{M1})}{v_1 - v_0} \tag{2}$$

In Eqs. (1) and (2), d represents the distance from the fault point to the local terminal (M-terminal), v_1 represents the linear mode wave velocity, v_0 represents the zero mode wave velocity, t_{M1} represents the time when the linear mode component reaches M, t_{M0} represents the time when the zero mode component reaches M, and Δt is the time difference between the initial traveling wave and the reflected wave of the fault point collected at the local terminal. The principle of the single-terminal method is simple and straightforward. Owing to the complex wiring mode and fault type of the power line, the reflection of the reflected wave at the fault point is quite different, and the ranging accuracy is poor.

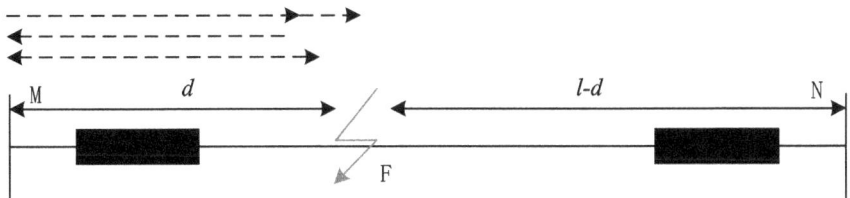

Fig. 2. The schematic diagram of single-terminal method.

3.2 Double-Terminal Method

The double-terminal method measures the distance by deploying monitoring equipment at both ends of the power line and using the time difference between the initial wave surge of the fault point and the monitoring point. This method can eliminate the impact of lightning strikes and the difference in parameters due to different line materials. This direction requires high accuracy of synchronous timing, dual channels, and high cost. Figure 3 shows a schematic of the double-terminal method.

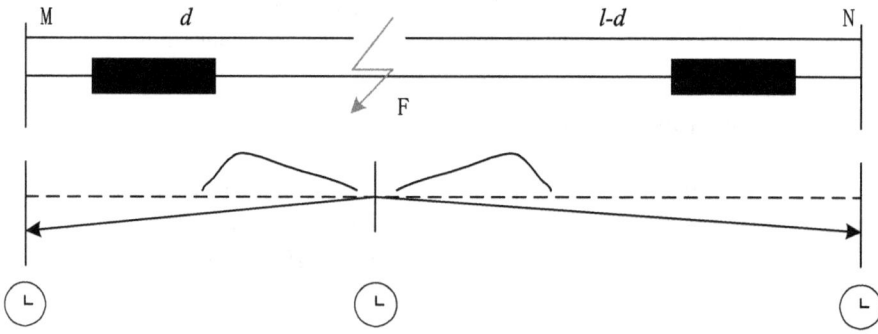

Fig. 3. The schematic diagram of double-terminal method.

Using the double-terminal positioning method, the fault point position can be calculated using the following formula.

$$d = \frac{1}{2}[l + v(t_M - t_N)] \tag{3}$$

In Eq. (3), the times of the fault point arrival and the cable line end and opposite end are represented.

3.3 Three-Terminal Method

The three-terminal method was improved based on the two-terminal method, and a fault location method was proposed. The fault location is determined by monitoring the absolute time t_M of the initial traveling wave of the fault point to the fault line (M-terminal), the absolute time t_N to the opposite end (N-terminal) and the absolute time t_P to the opposite end of the adjacent line (P-terminal). Figure 4 shows a schematic of the three-terminal method.

$$d = \frac{(t_M - t_N)l_2}{2(t_P - t_N)} + \frac{l_1}{2} \tag{4}$$

In Eq. (4), l_1 represents the distance from M-terminal to P-terminal, and l_2 represents the distance from the M-terminal to N-terminal.

The common problem is that in reality, the traveling wave will decay rapidly after two reflections or refractions, making the signal difficult to monitor.

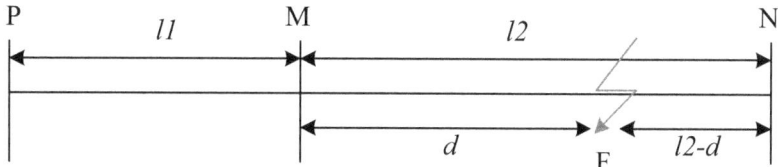

Fig. 4. The schematic diagram of three-terminal method.

4 Wavelet Transform

Wavelet transform is a time-scale analysis method that can characterize the local characteristics of signals in time and frequency domain. The wavelet transform can be divided into continuous and discrete wavelet transform. Continuous wavelet transform is more suitable for fault detection and classification in 10 kV distribution networks.

The quasi-voltages of the different wavelet scales are as follows:

$$U_a = U_s U_c / a \tag{5}$$

In Eq. (5), U_a represents the quasi-voltage, U_s represents the sampling voltage of the input signal, U_c represents the center voltage of the mother wavelet of the filtered wavelet, and a represents the scale factor of the wavelet.

The relationship between the wavelet coefficients and scale factors of the continuous wavelet transform is as follows:

$$|CWT(a, t)| \leq H a^\varepsilon \tag{6}$$

In Eq. (6), $CWT(a, t)$ is the continuous wavelet coefficient, H is the constant coefficient, a is the scale factor, and ε is the Nyquist index. The equality holds when $CWT(a, t)$ is the modulus maximum W_{mm}.

$$\log |W_{mm}(a)| = \log H + \varepsilon \log a \tag{7}$$

In Eq. (7), $\log a$ can be used as a variable, and $\log |W_{mm}(a)|$ can be used as a dependent variable, and there is a linear relationship between them.

The multi-scale wavelet transform has a strong denoising ability on a large scale and can roughly detect the signal mutation point, but the time accuracy is lacking. Although the signal mutation point can be accurately detected on a small scale, it is easily affected by noise. In this study, a multi-scale information fusion method was used to monitor the mutation point signal. The rough area of the mutation point is determined by the large scale, which can filter most of the noise interference, and then the location of the mutation point is accurately determined by the small scale.

5 Fault Diagnosis and Positioning Design

To realize the fault diagnosis and location of 10 kV power line based on wavelet transform, this study designs an online monitoring device integrated with wavelet transform. Figure 5 shows the fault diagnosis and location process of online monitoring device.

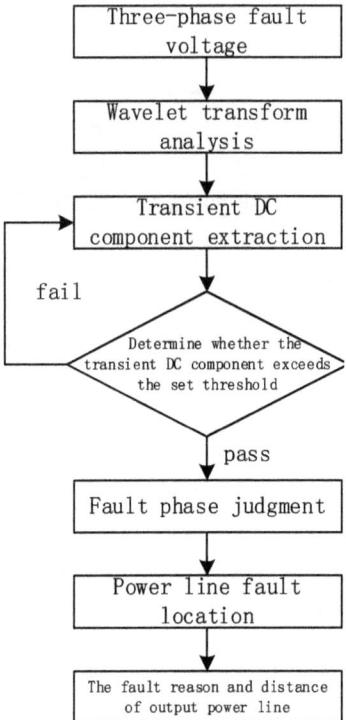

Fig. 5. Fault diagnosis and positioning process of online monitoring device.

Firstly, the online monitoring device collects the three-phase voltage of the power line when a fault occurs. Owing to the coupling relationship between the lines of the three-phase voltage, the wave velocity of the traveling wave cannot be determined. Therefore, the online monitoring device first decouples the three-phase voltage to improve the accuracy of the ranging. The α-mode component is obtained using Eq. (7) after the phase-mode transformation of the three-phase voltage at the fault moment, and then the α-mode component is transformed by wavelet. At this time, the accurate time when the initial traveling wave head reaches the online monitoring device on both sides can be obtained, and then the fault location can be accurately completed according to Eq. (3).

When the power line fails, the fault current can be decomposed into two parts: the AC component and decaying DC component. When the power line is in normal operation, owing to the possible three-phase imbalance of the line, the value of the decaying DC component is very small at this time; when the power line fails, the value of the decaying DC component will become larger, which is a quantity level higher than the DC component in normal operation. Based on this principle, the online monitoring device uses the value of the decaying DC component to locate the fault phase of the power line. Through the wavelet transform fault current, the effective extraction of the decaying DC component can be realized, and the fault phase of the power line can be determined. The fault phase determination strategy of the power line is as follows:

$$\begin{cases} |a_9|_A > TH, \text{A - phase fault} \\ |a_9|_B > TH, \text{B - phase fault} \\ |a_9|_C > TH, \text{C - phase fault} \end{cases} \quad (8)$$

In Eq. (8), $|a_9|_A$, $|a_9|_B$, and $|a_9|_C$ represent the initial value of the decaying DC component of phase A, B, and C, respectively, and TH represents the decision threshold. In Eq. (8), the initial values are less than the threshold value, indicating that the power line is in normal operation. If one of Eq. (8) is true, the online monitoring device marks the fault of the power line as a single-phase ground fault, and the fault phase is a phase exceeding the threshold. If the Eq. (8) has two items, the online monitoring device marks the fault of the power line as a two-phase short-circuit fault and then combines the zero-sequence component to determine whether it is grounded at this time. At this time, the fault phase is a two-phase that exceeds the threshold; if the three terms in Eq. (8) are valid, the online monitoring device marks the fault of the power line as a three-phase short-circuit fault. The threshold value should be selected based on the factors of the three-phase power line imbalance.

6 Experimental Verification and Analysis

To verify the correctness of the proposed method, a real environment of 10 kV single-ended radial distribution system was built, as shown in Fig. 6. R1 represents the resistance at the outlet end of the transformer. S1, S2, S3, S4, and S5 are 10 kV circuit breakers. F1, F2, and F3 are online monitoring devices. S2 and R2 were used to simulate phase-to-phase short-circuit faults. S3, R3, and C1 were used to simulate single-phase ground faults. LCC1 and LCC2 are line length impedance simulation loads, which can be adjusted by parameters. At the outlet end of 10 kV power supply, R1 was connected to S1, F1 was installed at S1, and then LCC1 was connected to LCC1. After LCC1, a fault simulation device is set up on the three-phase, and then F2 was installed, followed by S4 switch, LCC2, F3 and S5 were installed, and finally R4 was loaded through the line.

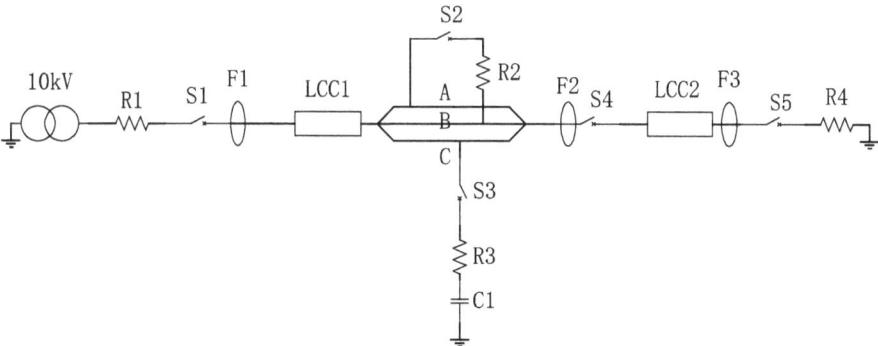

Fig. 6. True test circuit diagram.

Among them, the line current measurement accuracy of the online monitoring device is ±0.5%, the sampling rate of high-frequency voltage and current is 12.8 ksps, and the current amplitude, current harmonics, current direction and current imbalance can be collected. Simultaneously it has the historical filtering function of 1 h, and the fault diagnosis and positioning algorithm based on wavelet transform was integrated internally. In this study, only A, B two-phase short circuit and C-phase single-phase ground fault were selected for experiment, and the test process of other fault types is similar.

Table 1. A, B phase-to-phase short circuit fault prototype test results.

Power line fault location / km	4	8	14	19
$|a_9|_A$	1397.7	1423.6	1406.5	1413.3
$|a_9|_B$	1389.7	1411.6	1398.4	1391.8
$|a_9|_C$	47.9	50.3	48.5	49.2
Power line fault types	A, B phase-to-phase short circuit	A, B phase-to-phase short circuit	A, B phase-to-phase short circuit	A, B phase-to-phase short circuit
Location / km	4.085	8.088	14.092	19.093
positioning error / km	0.085	0.088	0.092	0.093
test result	correct	correct	correct	correct

It can be seen from the real test data in Table 1 that when the phase-to-phase short circuit occurs between phases A and B, the online monitoring device can correctly identify the fault type, and the maximum accuracy of fault location is 93 m, and the effect is good.

Table 2. True test results of C-phase single-phase ground fault.

Power line fault location / km	5.1	10.2	15.3	20.4
Transition resistance / Ω	0.01	0.01	0.01	0.01
$|a_9|_A$	50.2	49.6	50.1	49.7
$|a_9|_B$	49.8	49.9	49.5	49.3
$|a_9|_C$	695.7	698.3	670.1	697.2
Power line fault types	C phase grounding fault	C phase grounding fault	C phase grounding fault	C phase grounding fault
Location/km	5.174	10.276	15.390	20.488
positioning error/km	0.074	0.076	0.090	0.088

(*continued*)

Table 2. (*continued*)

Power line fault location / km	5.1	10.2	15.3	20.4
test result	correct	correct	correct	correct

Table 3. True test results of C-phase single-phase ground fault.

Power line fault location / km	5.1	10.2	15.3	20.4
Transition resistance / Ω	50.00	50.00	50.00	50.00
$|a_9|_A$	48.3	48.2	47.1	46.5
$|a_9|_B$	48.6	48.1	47.0	46.3
$|a_9|_C$	676.4	674.3	672.1	670.5
Power line fault types	C phase grounding fault	C phase grounding fault	C phase grounding fault	C phase grounding fault
Location / km	5.185	10.296	15.408	20.532
positioning error / km	0.085	0.096	0.108	0.132
test result	correct	correct	correct	correct

It can be seen from the real test data in Table 2 that when a metallic single-phase ground fault occurs in phase C, the online monitoring device can correctly identify the fault type, and the maximum accuracy of fault location is 90 m, and the effect is good. It can be seen from the real test data in Table 3 that when a non-metallic single-phase ground fault occurs in phase C, the online monitoring device can correctly identify the fault type, and the maximum accuracy of fault location is 132 m, and the effect is good.

7 Conclusions

This study analyzes the common fault types of power lines in 10 kV distribution networks, studies the fault location algorithm, designs the fault diagnosis and location strategy, and develops an online monitoring device for integrated power line fault diagnosis and location based on wavelet transform strategy. The reliability of the fault diagnosis and location method of the online monitoring device was verified by building a typical 10 kV single-ended radial distribution system. This method can effectively improve the accuracy and sensitivity of the fault location of the 10 kV distribution networks power line, and can ensure the safe and reliable operation of the power system.

References

1. Zheng, J., Chen, X., Qin, J., et al.: Field short-circuit test to validate travelling wave fault location using wavelet transform. Power Syst. Technol. **25**(3), 26–29 (2001)
2. Gao, J., Mu, X., Deng, L.: Simulation on signal location of cable fault point in power system. Comput. Simul. **34**(8), 151–156 (2017)
3. Guo, W., Wang, Y., Huang, C., et al.: Research on traveling wave ranging of transient arc breakdown faults in medium voltage cables. Power Syst. Clean Energy **40**(11), 31–38 (2024)
4. Cui, C., Wang, Z., Yang, D., et al.: Approach of fault location and fault-phase selection for transmission lines with wavelet transform. Control Eng. China **24**(S0), 85–91 (2017)
5. Hao, H.: Analysis of single phase ground fault in 10 kV low-resistance grounding system and countermeasures. Telecom Power Technol. **37**(3), 99–103 (2020)
6. Liu, Y., Yu, L., Lin, X., et al.: Interphase fault location method for distribution lines considering their parameter errors. Southern Power Syst. Technol. **18**(4), 141–151 (2024)

DMoE: A Semantic-Aware Engine with Mixture of Experts for Detecting Zero-Day Malware

Chenming Yang[1,2] and Kejiang Ye[2(✉)]

[1] Sangfor Technologies Inc., Shenzhen, China
yangchenming@sangfor.com.cn
[2] Shenzhen Institute of Advanced Technology, Chinese Academy of Sciences, Shenzhen, China
kj.ye@siat.ac.cn

Abstract. Zero-day malware represents a significant threat due to its novel attack vectors. Traditional detection mechanisms, which rely on predefined rules, often fail to identify these unprecedented techniques. Although dynamic analysis can expose malicious activities, most dynamic detection approaches lack the flexibility to detect zero-day malware due to the limited generalizability.

In response to these challenges, we introduce a new malware detection engine, DMoE, designed to identify zero-day malware by analyzing behavioral patterns using security knowledge. Since zero-day malware may obscure its malicious activities, DMoE conducts a multi-view examination of behaviors, encompassing API calls, registry modifications, file operations, process interactions, and network communications. DMoE achieves a balance between precision and generalizability during behavior representation: sensitive behavior matching for precision and semantic-aware representations enhanced by security knowledge for generalizability. We propose a heterogeneous Mixture of Experts (MoE) architecture, incorporating both inter-view and intra-view experts, further improving the capacity to represent complex behaviors.

Our evaluation of DMoE on a million-scale dataset composed of 11 malware categories demonstrates its superior performance over state-of-the-art methods. Moreover, when deployed an operational threat intelligence platform, DMoE detected over 100 zero-day malware within 2 weeks.

1 Introduction

Accurate and timely malware detection is a fundamental requirement in endpoint security. However, the computational resources at endpoints are often limited, leading anti-virus solutions to rely on extensive databases of known malware signatures and static heuristic rules to identify variants [31]. Malware authors, aware of these detection strategies, increasingly employ evasion tactics like packing, obfuscation, and encryption to construct zero-day malware for anti-detection

[30]. Consequently, zero-day malware poses a significant threat at a relatively low cost, particularly to enterprises and institutions [12].

The works focus on detecting malware can be classified into three categories [34]: static, dynamic, and hybrid. Traditional static detection methods rely on predefined static rules like YARA [4], which are derived from the typical features of known families as determined by malware analysts. In addition, machine learning models are used to identify malware by analyzing static attributes, including binary values [22] and function call graphs [5]. However, the effectiveness of static detection is often compromised by the ease with which adversaries can circumvent predefined rules or patterns [20], rendering these methods less capable of identifying novel malware variants.

Dynamic detection methods are based on dynamic behaviors during sandbox analysis. Techniques such as sequence analysis and graph analysis are employed to identify characteristic API call patterns associated with malware. However, detecting malware solely through API can obscure the understanding of function-level behavior, potentially resulting in false positives due to atypical API usage [29]. The limited set of behaviors and insufficient generalizability diminishes the efficacy of these methods against zero-day malware [12].

Given that zero-day malware can evade conventional detection methods, it is imperative to adopt the analytical paradigm employed by human security experts. Following the analysis paradigm of security experts, we design a malware detection engine, DMoE, which utilizes a multi-view approach encompassing API, registry, file, process, and network behaviors. This methodology is anticipated to yield a more thorough and precise detection capability than that of single-view detection systems. There are two major challenges, how to represent behavior with security knowledge and how to unify multiple views.

For challenge 1, since DMoE is a general malware detection engine, DMoE models behaviors in each view from two perspectives, transductive and inductive. The transductive approach focuses on the recognition of known patterns, enhancing the precision in identifying known malware and their simple variants. This is accomplished through sensitive behavior matching, a technique that discerns statistically or historically significant behavioral discrepancies between malware and benign software (greenware). For unseen behaviors that are absent from existing datasets, even security experts can only use security knowledge to understand them inductively. To ensemble security knowledge, DMoE encapsulates behaviors into data structures that are conducive to the application of the knowledge. More precisely, since API calls are general operations, we can get semantic description of the function of an API call from a LLM and encode the function description into numerical features. For other views of behaviors, entirely novel behaviors, such as the creation of new registry paths or files, are undertaken, we employ a specialized pre-training regimen for each behavioral perspective using Masked Language Modeling.

For Challenge 2, we develop a heterogeneous Mixture-of-Experts (MoE) [8,10,27] architecture to represent behaviors in different views and fuse them into the same space. For inter-view representation, we implement expert specialization [11] that each expert acquires non-overlapping and focused knowledge by Fine-Grained Expert Segmentation and Shared Expert Isolation. For intra-view representation, we adopt intra-view fusion among experts in different views. Given that behaviors exhibited in distinct views may indicate varying degrees of malicious intent, we apply cross-view attention gates to weight the behavior features accordingly, ensuring proper alignment within the feature space. This method of feature fusion empowers the classifier to identify malware with comprehensiveness and adaptability.

In summary, the contribution of this paper is as follows.

- We propose a new detection engine based on MoE architecture, which is capable of detecting highly-adversarial malware by multi-view behavior analysis informed by security knowledge.
- We design a new paradigm of representing behavior with knowledge by leveraging the semantic-ware knowledge embedding ability of language models, allowing known behavior matching and unknown behavior understanding.
- We implement behavior representation with a heterogeneous MoE architecture to enhance representation capacity.
- We evaluate DMoE on a real-world dataset with 4 million sandbox reports. The results validate the outperformance of DMoE on malware detection.
- We deploy DMoE on a practical threat intelligence platform and detect 137 zero-day malware that target on governments and financial institutions, which have escape from detection by most anti-virus products.

2 Background and Related Work

There are three major categories of malware detection methods classified with the utilized analysis techniques [1,34]: static, dynamic, and hybrid.

Numerous static analysis methods utilize a signature-based approach [23,24] to identify malicious file hashes or byte sequences. However, signature-based methods are inherently limited in detecting zero-day malware due to the absence of pre-existing signatures. [25]. To overcome this limitation, machine learning algorithms have been integrated into static analysis over recent decades. [3,26]. Static features like API and function call [2], strings [16], opcodes [13] and byte sequences [6] serve as inputs for machine learning models.

Dynamic analysis has gained popularity due to its ability to provide comprehensive and in-depth insights by executing malware within a sandbox. A sandbox constitutes a secure testing environment that allows samples to execute in isolation, thereby preventing contamination of external systems. To monitor the running behaviors of a sample, multiple probes are strategically placed within various logical components. The recorded behaviors include every API call and operations on registry, file, network, and process. These behaviors are systematically compiled into a structured data format within a sandbox report.

A primary focus of such analysis is the sequence of API calls, which plays a crucial role in the malware's interaction with the system. Attributes such as API name [7,9,14,35], argument [7,35], and frequency [14] are used, either singly or

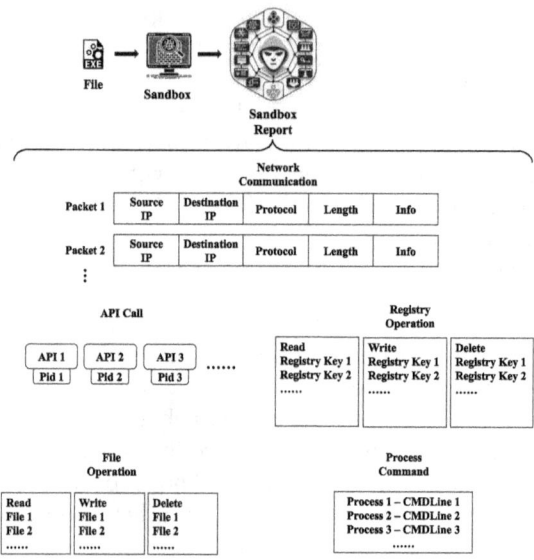

Fig. 1. The main views of behaviors and their original format in DMoE.

in combination, for behavioral modeling. Given the variability in API behavior formats, various feature engineering methods are employed, including feature hashing [35], API-Process graph [9], etc.

Hybrid analysis methods employ static features to complement dynamic features. In theory, hybrid analysis has the potential to outperform either static or dynamic analysis alone. Nevertheless, if there is a lack of alignment between static and dynamic features, machine learning models may suffer from performance degradation owing to feature interference.

3 Overview

DMoE is a malware detection engine based on dynamic analysis reports from a sandbox. The core idea of DMoE is to detect malicious behaviors from multiple views with the help of security knowledge in these views. To enhance the detection's comprehensiveness and accuracy, we utilize API, registry, file, process, and network.

To enable automated multi-view detection, each expert model processes and interprets behaviors within a specific view, aided by view-specific security knowledge. The DMoE comprises three primary components: (1) behavior preprocessing, (2) behavior representation based on multi-view MoE, and (3) the detection module. Figures 1, 2, 3, and 5 illustrate the architecture of DMoE and the workflow of the three components. Upon receiving a sandbox report, DMoE extracts behaviors from each view and converts them into model-readable data

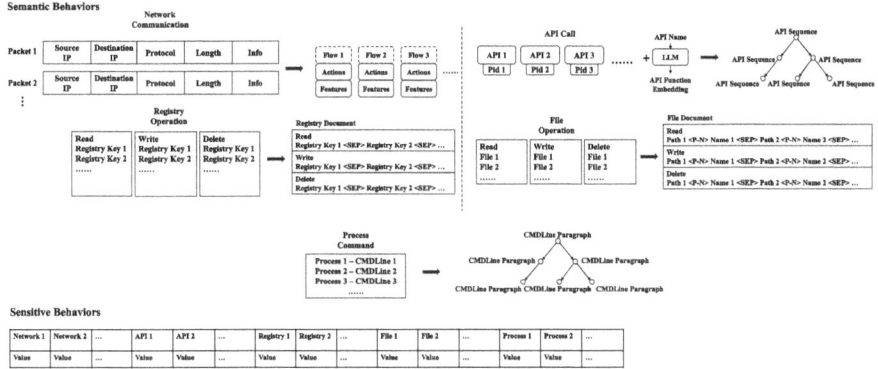

Fig. 2. The pre-processing of different views of behaviors.

via (1), represents the behaviors with domain-specific knowledge in each view and fuses them with (2), and detects malware based on classification by (3).

4 Design Details

In this section, we describe how DMoE works for malware detection. The architectures, operation procedures, and computation units of the four major components of DMoE are present in details.

4.1 Behavior Preprocess

Finding the optimal approach of behavior modelling is fundamental to malware detection. In DMoE, the modelled behaviors should must retain information essential for security analysts while excluding noise. Meanwhile, unlike the diverse data types humans can process, the modelled behaviors should also be machine-readable. We present the details of each view in the following.

API. The Cuckoo sandbox reports detail API logs that encompass four principal components: the API's designation, its arguments, the Process ID, and the corresponding timestamp. The nomenclature of most APIs is standardized across similar systems, with certain names encapsulating both the operations performed and the objects involved. The arguments vary in accordance with the API's specific functionality. For instance, the API *RegOpenKeyEx* signifies the action of opening a specific registry key; *NtCreatFile* creates a new file or directory, or opens an existing file, device, directory, or volume.

Considering the temporal and structural dependency of API calls, DMoE preprocesses the API records into API call sequence and API call dependence graph. It should be noted that API arguments are excluded here, because they are involved in a more fine-grained manner in other behavior views. For an API call sequence, each element is an API name, with the calls arranged chronologically by timestamp (API 1, API 2, ..., API N). For an API call dependence graph, each node signifies a process, each directed edge denotes a parent process calling a child process, and the node feature is the API call sequence in this process. Through the two pre-processing ways, DMoE can keep the overall API information in this sample, as well as the multi-process API information.

Registry and File. For registry, its key is a path that corresponds to some function and its value is the particular setting of that function. The *open*, *write*, and *delete* on registry are the advanced behaviors that can reflect malicious intent. Given the variability in registry key and value content, the application of static feature engineering methods may result in the loss of critical semantic information. For instance, "HKLM/Software/WowNode64/Run/" denotes the configuration on AutoRun, while "/Microsoft/Windows/CurrentVersion/Run/" signifies an analogous function.

To enable comprehensive and semantic understanding of registry behaviors, DMoE combines the key and the value and treats them as a sentence; then, multiple sentences are concatenated into a paragraph, as shown in Fig. 3. The preprocessing methodology for file behaviors parallels that of registry behaviors, wherein the file path, name, and type are integrated and conceptualized as sentences, which are subsequently merged to form paragraphs.

Process. The inter-dependence between multiple processes is contained in the API-process graph. Beyond mere dependencies, process directory, process name, and the executed commands (cmdLine) are also pivotal for deep analysis. These elements, formatted in natural language, contain a wealth of semantic information capable of unveiling behavioral anomalies. Excessive depth in the direct dependencies may indicate an attempt at process concealment; similarly, if a secondary process resides in a non-system directory while bearing the system-default process name 'svchost.exe', it may suggest an act of masquerading.

To preserve the semantic information of the processes, DMoE converts them into cmdline-process graph. Similar with the API-process graph, the graph structure is constructed from process dependency, while the node attribute is the (directory, name, cmdLine) in the sequence form.

Network. In an advanced sandbox, the network behaviors are recorded by a PCAP file that details packet-level traffic. In DMoE preprocessing, the traffic are aggregated into flows according to the protocols, including DNS, UDP, TCP, HTTP, and HTTPS. For each protocol, we choose multiple actions that can be related to malicious behaviors, such as DNS Query/Answer with type A/AAA/CNAME/MX... and the GET/POST action in HTTP. The detailed behaviors of the actions are recorded by features for specific actions. For example, the URL link in the HTTP GET action is the most important term to analyze and we leverage multiple features for URL analysis for these action, including host entropy, status code, link length, download type, file size, etc.

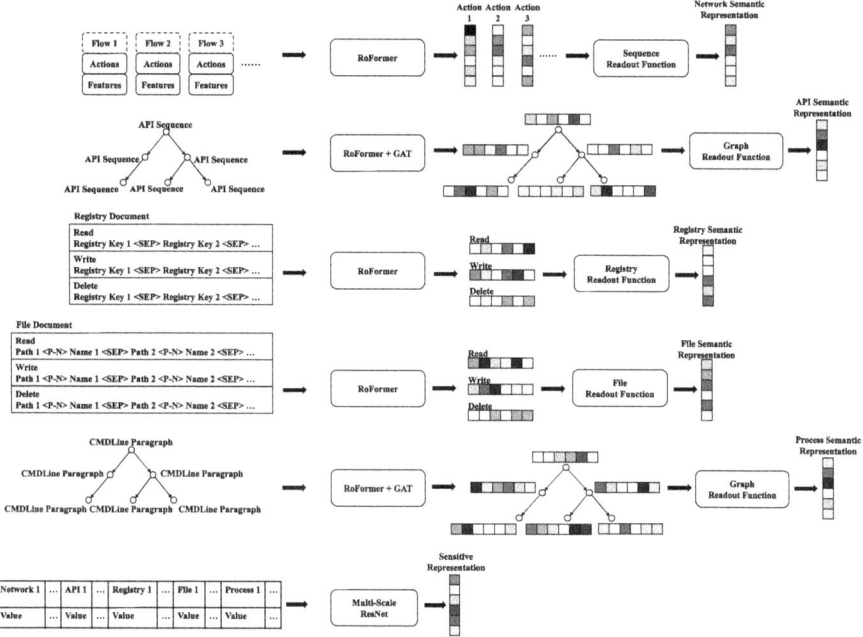

Fig. 3. Behavior representation of each view.

4.2 Behavior Representation in Each View

After behavior preprocessing, the original behaviors have been converted into machine-readable formats. In the following, we illustrate the details of how to represent the pre-processed behaviors into informative features, utilizing security knowledge pertinent to each perspective.

Sensitive Behavior Matching. Malware has been proliferating and evolving for decades, during which a substantial body of knowledge has accumulated. Within this historical knowledge base, certain behaviors stand out as particularly salient to security experts. These behaviors facilitate the detection of malware variants that have been altered from established malware templates.

In DMoE, we establish a database to store sensitive behavioral patterns derived from two principal sources: 1. Expert rules: used for anomaly detection; 2. Statistical rules: large frequency difference between malware and benign samples. For expert rules, we utilize both precise behaviors and heuristic behaviors. For statistical rules, we select 2 million malware and benign samples, and record the behaviors with high frequency.

Since there are sensitive behaviors from different views in the database, it is imperative to capture complex relations during representation. Therefore, we design a multi-scale representation module for each view of behaviors motivated, inspired by ResNet [15]. The module is composed of N branches with sandwich blocks that establish form a hierarchical structure.

Semantic-Aware Representation. Relying solely on historical accumulation of sensitive behaviors is insufficient for detecting zero-day malware. Motivated by the analytical methodology of security experts, it is essential to facilitate behavior comprehension based on security knowledge. We leverage the power of LLMs to obtain API description.

> **Prompt:** I hope you to act as an experienced security analysis expert with all the knowledge of Windows system. I will provide you an API call. You will write a brief and clear description on the function and usage of this API call. You should use all the knowledge of Windows system and all the experience of security analysis to derive the description. There is no need to tell me that it is a Windows API call. Do not include special tags like '\n', '\t'. The API call is xxx.
>
> xxx = NtClose
>
> **Answer:** NtClose is a low-level system function used to close object handles in Windows. It's part of the Native API and is typically called by higher-level Windows API functions (like CloseHandle). This function is crucial for resource management, as it releases system resources associated with the handle. Security analysts often monitor NtClose calls to track handle usage and potential handle leaks. Malware may abuse this function to close handles to critical system objects, potentially disrupting system operations or evading detection. Proper use of NtClose is essential for maintaining system stability and security, while its misuse can lead to resource exhaustion or system instability.
>
> xxx = RegQueryValueExW
> **Answer:** RegQueryValueExW is a Windows API function used to retrieve data from a specified registry value. It allows querying the type and content of a registry value in a given key. This function is commonly used by applications and system processes to read configuration settings, user preferences, or other stored data from the Windows Registry. Security analysts often monitor its usage to detect potential malware activities, such as attempts to access sensitive registry keys or modify system configurations. The function provides flexibility in retrieving various data types and can be used to enumerate registry values when combined with other registry functions.
>
> xxx = SetWindowsHookExW
> **Answer:** SetWindowsHookExW is a powerful Windows API function used to install an application-defined hook procedure into a hook chain. It allows developers to intercept and monitor system events, such as keyboard or mouse input, before they reach their intended target application. This function is commonly used for implementing keyboard listeners, system-wide hotkeys, or monitoring user interactions. However, it's also a potential vector for malicious activities like keylogging or intercepting sensitive information. Security analysts often scrutinize its usage in software to identify potential threats or unauthorized monitoring. Proper implementation and careful examination of code using this API are crucial for maintaining system security and user privacy.

Fig. 4. API function description from LLM.

Since most APIs are generally used in the system and the function descriptions are accessible online, we argue that API-related inquiries are safeguarded against "hallucination". Rather than directly asking the LLM about whether a API sequence is malicious, we focus on the API functions. The prompt is present in Fig. 4. For the 784 APIs that have appeared in our collected dataset, we record the function description for each API. Then, the function description is fed to a text embedding model to get its vector representation. Considering performance and efficiency, we utilize gte-Qwen2-7B-instruct [33], a model that achieves high-performance on massive text embedding benchmark [21], with embedding dimension 3584.

API Sequence/Network Action Sequence Representation

The knowledge-enhanced API sequence/Network Action Sequence is input to a sequence model to fuse security knowledge and temporal dependence. Since the temporal dependence is critical for presenting API behaviors, DMoE leverages RoFormer [28], a Transformer variant that improves position modeling ability by Rotary Position Embedding (RoPE).

API-Process Graph Representation

It is common in API analysis that only the combination of some API sequences of some processes presents anomalous patterns. DMoE employs a

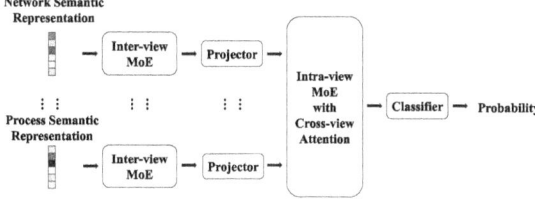

Fig. 5. The detection module of DMoE.

graph encoder module to accomplish this task. The basic computation block is the message-passing graph neural network (MPGNN). The message passing algorithm include three major procedures, edge message computing with $MSG(\cdot)$, node message aggregation with $AGG(\cdot)$, and feature update with $UDT(\cdot)$,

$$\begin{aligned} \mathbf{m}_{kj}^l &= MSG\left(\mathbf{h}_k^{l-1}, \mathbf{h}_j^{l-1}\right) \\ \mathbf{m}_k^l &= AGG\left(\{\mathbf{m}_{kj}^l | j \in \mathcal{N}_k\}\right) \\ \mathbf{h}_k^l &= UDT\left(\mathbf{h}_k^{l-1}, \mathbf{m}_k^l\right) \end{aligned} \quad (1)$$

where $\mathbf{h}_k^l$ is the feature of node k at the l-th layer of MPGNN, $\mathcal{N}_k$ denotes the set of 1-hop neighbors of node k. For expressiveness and efficiency, DMoE employs graph attention (GAT) network [32] with some modification as the node-level graph encoder.

Registry, File, and CmdLine as Paragraph. In the context of registry, file, and command-line behaviors, the manifestations can be highly variable, with the potential for novel instances. To address this, we employ pre-training and fine-tuning of specialized language models to interpret such behaviors effectively. Our primary goal is to develop a paragraph embedding model; hence, we utilize RoBERTa [19], renowned for its capability in paragraph-level comprehension.

Since there is no existing pre-trained model of Roberta for registry, file, and cmdLine, we pre-train three models for each view. We take registry as the example to illustrate the training process. The structure of a registry entry, as depicted in Fig. 2, is processed such that each sub-directory is regarded as an individual token within a sequence. After pre-training, the encoder of the Roberta model is repurposed as a feature extractor for registry understanding.

4.3 Detection

View Fused Classifier. After getting basic representations for each view of behaviors, it is necessary to enhance their representation capacity and fuse them effectively for classification. To achieve the two goals, we design a heterogeneous MoE architecture from inter-view and intra-view perspectives.

The inter-view MoE, as shown in Fig. 6, aims to augment the representational capacity of each view. This architecture includes multiple experts that are implemented with MLPs and a routing gate for selecting the most capable expert for

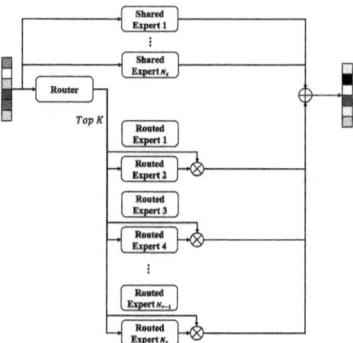

Fig. 6. Intra-view MoE with shared experts and Top K routing.

the current prediction. Each expert is designed to handle specific knowledge that are useful for the task, analogous to the varied expertise found among human specialists. The requirement of experts specialization, i.e. each expert acquires non-overlapping and focused knowledge, is fulfilled by using fine-grained expert segmentation and shared expert isolation in [11]. Through the two techniques, the representation capacity can be greatly enhanced.

The intra-view MoE is adopted to adaptively select useful behavior features in different views. The selection should be conducted in the same feature space, so we design a behavior alignment module through feature concatenation and projection. After alignment, the features in different views $\mathbf{H} = (\mathbf{h}_1, \ldots, \mathbf{h}_N)$ are input to a cross-view attention gate,

$$\mathbf{H}_{att} = softmax(\frac{\mathbf{H}\mathbf{W}_Q \mathbf{W}_K^\top \mathbf{H}}{\sqrt{(d_K)}})\mathbf{H}\mathbf{W}_V \tag{2}$$

where $\mathbf{W}_Q, \mathbf{W}_K, \mathbf{W}_V$ are the weight matrices of query, key, and value.

After intra-view MoE, the behaviors in all views are aligned and fused. The representations are then input to a MLP classifier for comprehensive detection, which outputs the malicious probability of each sample.

Training Paradigm. The training paradigm of DMoE follows the standard supervised classification. DMoE can be used for malware detection and malware classification, which are modeled as binary classification and multi-class classification respectively.

Specifically, for multi-class classification task, we turn it into multiple binary classification tasks. The main reason is that the classifier can be overconfident about the prediction. For example, a RAT may also be infected by a Worm, and present behaviors of both families. Both labels are true labels, but only one is preferred during training, leading to information loss. Forcing the model to classify this sample into RAT can cause behavior bias, which acts as a dirty sample. In multiple binary classification, since overconfidence in one class will not influence other classes, the information loss will be reduced.

Table 1. Overall performance of different methods.

Methods	Feature	FPR	FNR	Precision	Recall	F1-Score	AUC
DMalNet	API	0.1375	0.1263	0.8830	0.8737	0.8783	0.8713
BiLSTM	API	0.1687	0.1667	0.8511	0.8333	0.8421	0.8375
CruParamer	API	0.1039	0.1075	0.9121	0.8925	0.9022	0.9134
DPNSA	Bytes	0.1375	0.0667	0.8991	0.9333	0.9159	0.9209
API2Vec	API & Process	0.0676	0.0769	0.9438	0.9231	0.9333	0.9370
FewM-HGCL	Hybrid	0.0191	0.0406	0.9793	0.9594	0.9692	0.9724
DMoE	Hybrid	0.0122	0.0152	0.9873	0.9848	0.9861	0.9911

5 Evaluation

In this section, we present the implementation and evaluation of DMoE on a large malware detection dataset. Then, we provide the results of DMoE on zero-day malware detection in real-world deployment and ablation study.

5.1 Dataset

We collect sandbox reports of malware and benign samples on a threat intelligence (TI) platform. This platform employs multiple sandbox instances operating in parallel to enhance efficiency. To enable acceptable analysis delay, each sample is run for up to 5 min.

In this dataset, we select executable files (.exe) in Windows and the operation system in the sandbox is Windows 10. To construct a class-balanced dataset, we select 2000000 samples with effective behaviors for malware and benign samples respectively. Moreover, to mirror real-world conditions, our selection of malware samples encompassed diverse categories, including Trojans, Worms, Viruses, Backdoors, Infostealers, Hacktools, CoinMiners, Ransomware, Downloaders, Droppers, Spyware, and Adware. This variety ensures that the DMoE model is exposed to a broad spectrum of malicious behaviors.

Following the standard configuration in supervised learning, the dataset is split into training, validation, and test parts with 70%:15%:15%. The learnable model parameters are tuned on the training set, and the hyperparameters are adjusted on the validation set. For performance comparison, we evaluate their ability to correctly classify malware and benign samples on the test set.

To evaluate the performance on zero-day malware, we also construct a small test dataset that has 1000 malware samples using advanced adversarial techniques. Most of these samples are Backdoor, Infostealer, and RAT. The malware samples are double-justified by security experts and VirusTotal.

5.2 Effectiveness

For comprehensive comparison, we adopt False Positive Rate (FPR), False Negative Rate (FNR), Precision, Recall, F1-score, and area under the ROC curve

(AUC) scores as the evaluation metrics. We conduct the experiments for 10 times with random seeds on data splits and model training, and record the average results for fair comparison.

Performance Comparison. Table 1 presents the detailed performance of DMoE and the compared baselines, including DMalNet [17], BiLSTM [35], CruParamer [7], DPNSA [6], API2Vec [9], FewM-HGCL [18], on the malware detection dataset with default threshold 0.5. DMoE achieves the best performance among all baseline models, and outperforms the best-performed baseline FewM-HGCL by 5.5%. Among the evaluated methods, we can see that detection methods based on more than one view perform apparently better than single-view detection methods.

Since false positives can adversely affect normal operation of user system, maintaining a low FP rate is a fundamental requirement for anti-virus engines. Therefore, a well-performed anti-virus engine should have high recall rate. Figure 7 summarizes the Recall rates at varying FP rates of $\{0.1, 0.01, 0.001, 0.005, 0.0001\}$ by adjusting the detection threshold. DMoE consistently outperforms other baselines across all different FP rates. Notably, at an FP rate of 0.0001—a threshold highly desirable in FP-sensitive environments—DMoE's performance exceeds that of the best-performing baseline by over 50%.

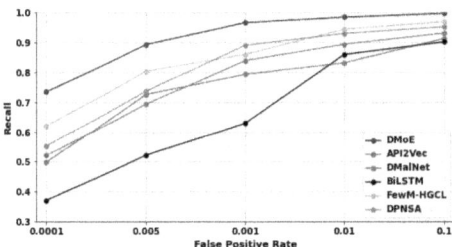

Fig. 7. Recall of different methods on the total malware dataset.

To more rigorously assess detection ability on zero-day malware, we conduct experiments on the small test set that uses highly adversarial techniques and is confirmed by malware analysis experts. The Recall rates for different FP rates are included in Fig. 8. We observe that the outperformance of DMoE is more apparent even for high FP rate like 0.1 and 0.01, and keep high detection performance for low FP rate scenarios. Moreover, since FewM-HGCL that uses hybrid views of behaviors also performs better, this validates the effectiveness of multi-view behavior modeling.

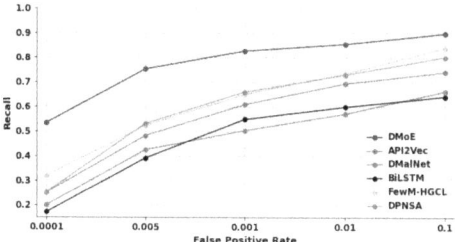

Fig. 8. Recall of different methods on highly adversarial malware dataset.

5.3 Zero-Day Malware Detection

We deploy DMoE as a standalone detection module subsequent to the cloud sandbox on a Threat Intelligence platform. The malware detection architecture is composed of static detection engines and dynamic detection engines. We perform preliminary filtering by selecting recently compiled samples, and focus on those detected by few static engines.

According to analysis by security experts, 138 zero-day malware are detected by DMoE. These samples exhibited various static adversarial tactics, such as sophisticated packing, code obfuscation, and the retrieval of payloads from remote servers. Among the zero-day malware, there are 10 samples that are new variants of the Gh0st family in RAT. We also find a new attack method that utilizes the signature vulnerability of a widely-used software for security monitoring. The attacker replaces the IP address for monitoring with C2 IP address and transmits shellcode through this address. Since the malware has legal digital signature, the signature-based detection products cannot declare it as malicious.

To evaluate the performance of DMoE on zero-day malware, we upload the 138 samples to VirusTotal and collect the detection results in Table 2. It can be seen that these zero-day malware can escape from detection by most engines.

Table 2. The number of detected engines on VirusTotal.

Total	VT: 0-1	VT: 2-5	VT: 5-10	VT: 10+
138	41	35	39	25

5.4 Ablation Study

We now analyze the impact of key components on the effectiveness of DMoE. The primary claim of our work is the importance of utilizing multiple views of behaviors. To validate this claim, we conduct multiple experiments by removing each view from DMoE and the results are summarized in Table 3. Removing each view would cause performance degradation by 1%-17.6%. Among all views, removing the API behavior lead to the most substantial impact by 17.6%, which coincides with the common security knowledge that API calls are the basic behavior of a sample. We also test the necessity of encoding security knowledge into API behavior modeling. It can be seen that removing the functional knowledge of API calls, the performance degrades by 3%. The degradation is enlarged to 7% on the 138 zero-day malware.

Table 3. Effect of different components on DMoE's performance

Component	Precision	Recall	F1-Score	AUC
network	0.9855	0.9624	0.9738	0.9794
API	0.8317	0.8206	0.8261	0.8165
API function	0.9593	0.9628	0.9610	0.9608
registry	0.9642	0.9448	0.9544	0.9586
file	0.9719	0.9683	0.9701	0.9731
process	0.9828	0.9316	0.9565	0.9432
DMoE	0.9873	0.9848	0.9861	0.9911

We also evaluate the impact of some hyper-parameter choices. The number of experts in inter-view MoE is set in $\{1, 2, 4, 6, 8\}$, and the ratio of utilized training set is set from 0.1 to 1.0. Figure 9 and Fig. 10 show the experimental results. In general, the growth of expert number will lead to more model parameters and DMoE performs better when it grows from 1 to 4. For different choices of training ratios, the performance goes up from 0.2 to 0.6 significantly, while keeps stable from 0.8 to 1.0.

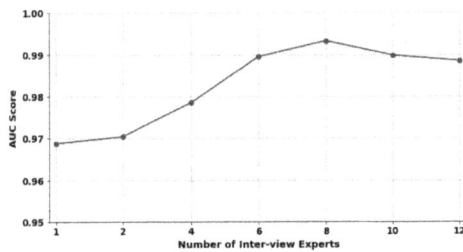

Fig. 9. Effect of the number of experts on DMoE's performance

5.5 Efficiency

We measure the runtime efficiency of DMoE, including data processing, training, and inference. Since DMoE adopts early stopping during training, we conclude

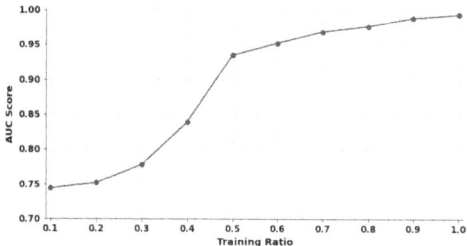

Fig. 10. Effect of utilized ratio of training set on DMoE's performance

the average training time for 10 random seeds. There are two modes of measuring inference, stream mode and batch mode. Compared with steam mode, batch mode infers several samples asynchronously, and the batch size is set to $\{10, 20, 50, 80\}$ restricted by the GPU memory. The results are listed in Table 4.

Table 4. Overhead of each stage.

Stage	Average Time Consumption
preprocessing	0.15 sec/sample
pre-training	18.1 h
training	38.6 h
inference (stream)	0.24 sec/sample
inference (batch size = 10)	0.21 sec/sample
inference (batch size = 20)	0.19 sec/sample
inference (batch size = 50)	0.16 sec/sample
inference (batch size = 80)	0.19 sec/sample

Benefit from parallel processing, the average time of data processing for each sample is 0.15 s. DMoE takes 38.6 h in average for training 11 epochs, and the pre-training of semantic-ware representation models needs 18.1 h in average. The evaluation of runtime efficiency is conducted under no strategy for training acceleration. The overhead can be reduced if acceleration methods for gradient processing are employed.

In stream mode, the inference time per sample is 0.24 s. In batch mode, this time decreases almost linearly with increasing batch sizes of 10,20,50, but encounters a bottleneck as the batch size continues to increase. This is primarily because GPU memory is exhausted at a batch size of 80, which affects computational efficiency due to tensor caching. Overall, these results suggest that DMoE is capable of detecting malware in near real-time.

6 Conclusion

In this work, we present DMoE, a new engine based on MoE architecture that can detect zero-day malware from multi-view dynamic behaviors. DMoE employs a semantic-aware approach to incorporate security knowledge into behavior representation, facilitated by a heterogeneous MoE architecture that enhances the understanding of complex behaviors. Our evaluation, conducted on a large-scale dataset, indicates that DMoE surpasses contemporary state-of-the-art methods and products in malware detection, achieving superior performance with a low false positive rate. Furthermore, the deployment of DMoE in real-world scenarios has demonstrated its significant capability to detect zero-day malware.

References

1. Aboaoja, F.A., Zainal, A., Ghaleb, F.A., Al-Rimy, B.A.S., Eisa, T.A.E., Elnour, A.A.H.: Malware detection issues, challenges, and future directions: a survey. Appl. Sci. **12**(17), 8482 (2022)
2. Al-Dujaili, A., Huang, A., Hemberg, E., O'Reilly, U.M.: Adversarial deep learning for robust detection of binary encoded malware. In: 2018 IEEE Security and Privacy Workshops (SPW), pp. 76–82. IEEE (2018)
3. Alraizza, A., Algarni, A.: Ransomware detection using machine learning: a survey. Big Data Cogn. Comput. **7**(3), 143 (2023)
4. Alvarez, V.M.: Yara – the pattern matching swiss knife for malware researchers. https://virustotal.github.io/yara/ (2020)
5. Bilot, T., El Madhoun, N., Al Agha, K., Zouaoui, A.: A survey on malware detection with graph representation learning. ACM Comput. Surv. **56**(11), 1–36 (2024)
6. Chai, Y., Du, L., Qiu, J., Yin, L., Tian, Z.: Dynamic prototype network based on sample adaptation for few-shot malware detection. IEEE Trans. Knowl. Data Eng. **35**(5), 4754–4766 (2022)
7. Chen, X., et al.: CruParamer: learning on parameter-augmented API sequences for malware detection. IEEE Trans. Inf. Forensics Secur. **17**, 788–803 (2022)
8. Clark, A., et al.: Unified scaling laws for routed language models. In: International Conference on Machine Learning, pp. 4057–4086. PMLR (2022)
9. Cui, L., Cui, J., Ji, Y., Hao, Z., Li, L., Ding, Z.: API2Vec: learning representations of API sequences for malware detection. In: Proceedings of the 32nd ACM SIGSOFT International Symposium on Software Testing and Analysis, pp. 261–273 (2023)
10. Dai, D., et al.: DeepSeekMoE: Towards ultimate expert specialization in mixture-of-experts language models. arXiv preprint arXiv:2401.06066 (2024)
11. DeepSeek-AI: DeepSeek-V2: A strong, economical, and efficient mixture-of-experts language model (2024)
12. Deldar, F., Abadi, M.: Deep learning for zero-day malware detection and classification: a survey. ACM Comput. Surv. **56**(2), 1–37 (2023)
13. Gao, X., Hu, C., Shan, C., Liu, B., Niu, Z., Xie, H.: Malware classification for the cloud via semi-supervised transfer learning. J. Inf. Secur. Appl. **55**, 102661 (2020)
14. Hansen, S.S., Larsen, T.M.T., Stevanovic, M., Pedersen, J.M.: An approach for detection and family classification of malware based on behavioral analysis. In: 2016 International Conference on Computing, Networking and Communications (ICNC), pp. 1–5. IEEE (2016)

15. He, K., Zhang, X., Ren, S., Sun, J.: Deep residual learning for image recognition. In: Proceedings of the IEEE Conference on Computer Vision and Pattern Recognition, pp. 770–778 (2016)
16. Kim, C., Chang, S.Y., Kim, J., Lee, D., Kim, J.: Automated, reliable zero-day malware detection based on autoencoding architecture. IEEE Trans. Netw. Serv. Manage. **20**(3), 3900–3914 (2023)
17. Li, C., et al.: DMalNet: dynamic malware analysis based on API feature engineering and graph learning. Comput. Secur. **122**, 102872 (2022)
18. Liu, C., Li, B., Zhao, J., Zhen, Z., Liu, X., Zhang, Q.: FewM-HGCL: few-shot malware variants detection via heterogeneous graph contrastive learning. IEEE Transactions on Dependable and Secure Computing (2022)
19. Liu, Y., et al.: RoBERTa: a robustly optimized BERT pretraining approach. In: International Conference on Learning Representations (2020)
20. Lucas, K., Pai, S., Lin, W., Bauer, L., Reiter, M.K., Sharif, M.: Adversarial training for {Raw-Binary} malware classifiers. In: 32nd USENIX Security Symposium (USENIX Security 23), pp. 1163–1180 (2023)
21. Muennighoff, N., Tazi, N., Magne, L., Reimers, N.: MTEB: massive text embedding benchmark. In: Proceedings of the 17th Conference of the European Chapter of the Association for Computational Linguistics, pp. 2014–2037 (2023)
22. Raff, E., Fleshman, W., Zak, R., Anderson, H.S., Filar, B., McLean, M.: Classifying sequences of extreme length with constant memory applied to malware detection. In: Proceedings of the AAAI Conference on Artificial Intelligence. vol. 35, pp. 9386–9394 (2021)
23. Rohini, S., Ramesh, G., Nair, A.R.: MAGIC: malware behaviour analysis and impact quantification through signature co-occurrence and regression. Comput. Secur. **139**, 103735 (2024)
24. Sathyanarayan, V.S., Kohli, P., Bruhadeshwar, B.: Signature generation and detection of malware families. In: Mu, Y., Susilo, W., Seberry, J. (eds.) ACISP 2008. LNCS, vol. 5107, pp. 336–349. Springer, Heidelberg (2008). https://doi.org/10.1007/978-3-540-70500-0_25
25. Scott, J.: Signature based malware detection is dead. Institute for Critical Infrastructure Technology (2017)
26. Shalaginov, A., Banin, S., Dehghantanha, A., Franke, K.: Machine learning aided static malware analysis: A survey and tutorial. Cyber threat intelligence, pp. 7–45 (2018)
27. Shazeer, N., et al.: Outrageously large neural networks: The sparsely-gated mixture-of-experts layer. arXiv preprint arXiv:1701.06538 (2017)
28. Su, J., Ahmed, M., Lu, Y., Pan, S., Bo, W., Liu, Y.: RoFormer: enhanced transformer with rotary position embedding. Neurocomputing **568**, 127063 (2024)
29. Suciu, O., Coull, S.E., Johns, J.: Exploring adversarial examples in malware detection. In: 2019 IEEE Security and Privacy Workshops (SPW), pp. 8–14. IEEE (2019)
30. Tong, L., Li, B., Hajaj, C., Xiao, C., Zhang, N., Vorobeychik, Y.: Improving robustness of {ML} classifiers against realizable evasion attacks using conserved features. In: 28th USENIX Security Symposium (USENIX Security 19), pp. 285–302 (2019)
31. Tounsi, W., Rais, H.: A survey on technical threat intelligence in the age of sophisticated cyber attacks. Comput. Secur. **72**, 212–233 (2018)
32. Veličković, P., Cucurull, G., Casanova, A., Romero, A., Lio, P., Bengio, Y.: Graph attention networks. arXiv preprint arXiv:1710.10903 (2017)
33. Yang, A., et al.: Qwen2 technical report. arXiv preprint arXiv:2407.10671 (2024)

34. Ye, Y., Li, T., Adjeroh, D., Iyengar, S.S.: A survey on malware detection using data mining techniques. ACM Comput. Surv. (CSUR) **50**(3), 1–40 (2017)
35. Zhang, Z., Qi, P., Wang, W.: Dynamic malware analysis with feature engineering and feature learning. In: Proceedings of the AAAI Conference on Artificial Intelligence. vol. 34, pp. 1210–1217 (2020)

Research on the Bidding Game Model of Clean Energy Power in Qinghai Evolution Province Based on Phased Network

Wen Yanyan[1(✉)], Zhang Jisheng[2], and Wang Baoqi[3]

[1] School of Business, Qinghai Institute of Technology, Xining, China
`1501374463@qq.com`
[2] Qinghai Ecological Environment Science Education and Publicity Center, Xining, China
[3] School of Economics and Management, Qinghai Nationalities University, Xining, China

1 Introduction

The clean energy industry in Qinghai Province has developed rapidly in recent years, and the network of cooperation among enterprises has evolved accordingly. Based on the evolution of the cooperative network of clean energy enterprises in Qinghai Province, this paper proposes an improved power bidding model, and combines game theory to analyze the evolution of enterprise bidding strategies at each stage and their long-term effects.

1.1 Literature Review

In recent years, research on clean energy power bidding has been increasing, especially in the combination of complex networks and game theory. The application of complex networks in electricity markets has received extensive attention because the cooperative networks among power companies directly affect their bidding strategies (Jiang et al., 2020). Multiple studies have shown that a company's position in the cooperative network, such as degree centrality and intermediary centrality, determines its dominance in electricity bidding (Wang et al., 2019).

Furthermore, game theory has been proven to be an effective tool for analyzing corporate behavior in the electricity market. Through game theory models, the strategy adjustment process of enterprises during the bidding process can be simulated, and the long-term benefits of different bidding strategies can be analyzed (Zhang & Li, 2021). Some studies suggest that cooperative strategies tend to produce more stable returns, while competitive strategies, although they may bring high returns in the short term, typically have less stable long-term returns (Li et al., 2022).

In the clean energy sector, especially in the electricity market dominated by renewable energy, the cooperative relationships and game-playing behaviors among enterprises are more complex. These co-operations involve not only traditional power supply chains but also external factors such as policy incentives and subsidies (Liu et al., 2020). In the field of electricity bidding and clean energy, the combination of game theory and complex networks has become a research hotspot. In recent years, several studies have shown that game theory has a significant advantage in analyzing the behavior of independent players in the electricity market, especially with the participation of renewable energy, where power generators have achieved remarkable results in optimizing bidding strategies through two-level game models (Jing Ling et al., 2017). In addition, complex network analysis has been applied to competition and cooperation in the electricity market, particularly in the retail electricity market, where studies have shown that network size, user switching behavior, and contract transactions have a significant impact on the pricing strategy of electricity retailers (Xinyi Xie et al., 2022). In the renewable energy market, game theory has also been used to analyze trading strategies between traditional Power plants and renewable energy producers, promoting the consumption of green power and market stability through optimizing trading strategies (Guangxi Power Exchange Center, 2024).

2 Network Evolution and Parameter Analysis at Different Stages

The cooperative network of clean energy enterprises in Qinghai Province evolved in four stages. In each stage, there are significant changes in the number of enterprises and cooperative relationships. This paper assesses the network position of enterprises in the bidding process and their potential bidding influence in each stage by calculating indicators such as degree centrality, intermediary centrality, and proximity centrality.

2.1 The First Stage

In Phase 1, there are 17 enterprises and 122 partnerships. Through game simulation, it was found that the bidding strategies of enterprises were relatively simple in the early stage, but due to the small and tight cooperative network, enterprises gradually reached a stable combination of bidding strategies, and the returns tended to stabilize.

2.2 The Second Stage

The network in Phase 2 expanded to 79 businesses and 1,705 partnerships. As the network expanded, the complexity of the bidding strategy increased, and the cooperative and competitive relationships among enterprises became more diverse. Game simulations showed greater fluctuations in returns, and eventually the strategy gradually stabilized.

2.3 The Third Stage

The network in Phase 3 expands further to 108 businesses and 3,236 partnerships. As the network becomes more complex, companies' bidding strategies need to be adjusted frequently, and game simulations show that companies constantly revise their strategies in multiple rounds of bidding to eventually form stable bidding results.

2.4 The Fourth Stage

In Phase 4, the network expands to 136 businesses and 5,032 partnerships. Although the network became more complex and the bidding behavior of enterprises showed more variations, the game simulation results indicated that after several rounds of bidding, the strategies of enterprises gradually stabilized and the returns remained at a relatively stable level.

3 An Improved Power Bidding Game Model

The improved power bidding game model proposed in this paper combines game theory with the process of network evolution. At each stage, the enterprise adjusts the bidding strategy based on the centrality indicator in its network, taking advantage of its network location to optimize the bidding results. The game simulation results show that the network structure at different stages has a significant impact on the long-term earnings and strategic stability of enterprises.

4 Results of Game Analysis at Each Stage and Long-Term Effects

4.1 Game Analysis in the First Stage

In the first stage, the cooperative network is smaller and tighter, and the adjustment of the enterprise's bidding strategy is relatively simple. Through game simulation, it can be seen that the earnings of enterprises fluctuate less in the early stage of the bidding and tend to stabilize quickly. This means that enterprises are more likely to form a consistent bidding strategy at this stage, the stability of the cooperative network is stronger, and in the long term, the profits of enterprises are relatively stable.

4.2 The Second Stage Game Analysis

As the network expands to the second stage, the number of enterprises and partnerships increases significantly, and so does the complexity of the bidding strategy. The game simulation shows that the earnings of enterprises fluctuate greatly in the early stage of the bidding and then gradually stabilize, indicating that enterprises need to gradually adjust their strategies through multiple rounds of bidding. This complex network of cooperation has a significant impact on long-term earnings, but eventually a relatively stable bidding strategy can be found.

4.3 The Third Stage Game Analysis

In the third stage, the complexity of the network structure increases further, and competition among enterprises intensifies. Game simulation results show that companies need to frequently adjust their strategies during the bidding process, and the volatility of earnings increases significantly. Although the earnings eventually stabilize, the long-term earnings of enterprises at this stage may be affected by greater uncertainty due to the complexity of the network.

4.4 Game Analysis in Stage 4

In the fourth stage, the cooperative network expands to its maximum scale, and the connections between enterprises are the most complex. The game simulation results indicated that the frequency of strategy adjustments by enterprises increased, and the earnings fluctuated significantly. Although the final strategy tends to stabilize, due to the large and complex scale of the network, the stability of long-term earnings is relatively low. At this stage, the company's bidding strategy needs to be more flexible to deal with more competition and partnerships.

5 Game Models and Parametric Analysis

In order to better simulate the behavior of clean energy enterprises in Qinghai Province during the electricity bidding process, this paper introduces a bidding model based on game theory. The model assumes that each enterprise has two strategy options during the bidding process: high bid or low bid. Enterprises adjust their bidding strategies based on their position in the cooperative network, the strategies of their partners, and their own historical performance. Through multiple rounds of play, each enterprise constantly adjusts its strategy to maximize its earnings.

5.1 Revenue Function

In the game, the earnings of each enterprise are directly related to its strategy choices and the strategies of its partners. Specifically, the revenue function of an enterprise can be expressed as: if the enterprise chooses a strategy similar to that of its partner (such as offering the same high price), its revenue will be higher. Conversely, if a company chooses a strategy contrary to that of its partner (such as the partner offering a low price and the company offering a high price), its earnings will decrease.

5.2 Parameter Analysis

In game models, the structure of the cooperative network has a significant impact on the bidding strategy and revenue of enterprises. By analyzing network parameters such as Degree Centrality, Betweenness Centrality, and Closeness Centrality, We can see how a firm's position in the cooperative network affects its strategy adjustments during the bidding process. Enterprises with high degree centrality tend to have more partners and thus dominate the bidding process. Enterprises with high mediating centrality play a key role in the flow of information and can influence the outcome of the bidding by controlling the flow of information.

6 Simulation Results of Different Cooperation Strategies

In this section, we simulate the impact of two different bidding strategies on corporate earnings: cooperative strategy and competitive strategy. Under the cooperative strategy, the company coordinates the bidding with its partners and adopts a consistent bidding strategy to maximize the common benefits. Under the competitive strategy, the firm bids independently, attempting to achieve higher returns by taking the opposite bidding behavior from its partners.

6.1 Analysis of Simulation Results

It can be seen from the simulation results that enterprises adopting cooperative strategies have relatively stable returns during the bidding process. By coordinating strategies with partners, companies formed relatively consistent bidding behaviors after multiple rounds of bidding, with less volatility in earnings and eventually stabilizing. In contrast, companies that adopt competitive strategies have greater earnings fluctuations in the early stages, and they adjust their strategies more frequently when attempting to achieve higher earnings through reverse strategies. Eventually, although they also tend to stabilize, their average earnings are lower than those of cooperative strategies.

6.2 Illustration of the Simulation Results

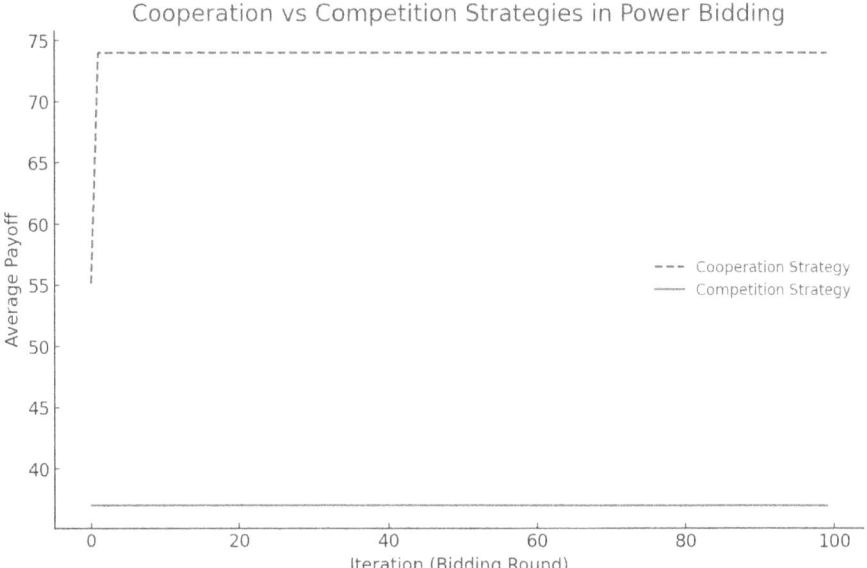

7 Analysis of Simulation Results for Different Parameters

In this section, we observe the impact on the bidding process by adjusting the distribution of the enterprise's initial bidding strategy. In the two simulation scenarios, 60 percent and 40 percent of the enterprises chose the high-bid strategy in the initial stage, respectively. We analyzed the impact on the stability of earnings by comparing the distributions of these two different initial strategies.

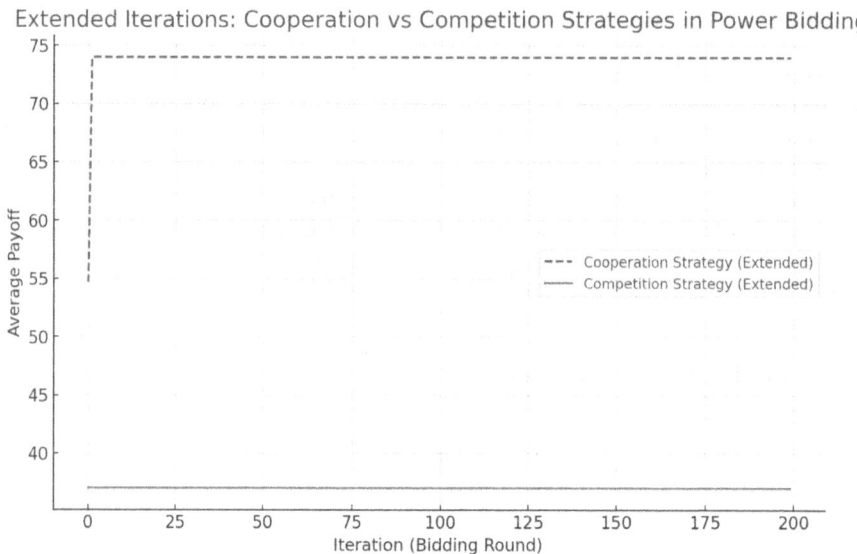

7.1 The Impact of Different Initial Strategy Distributions

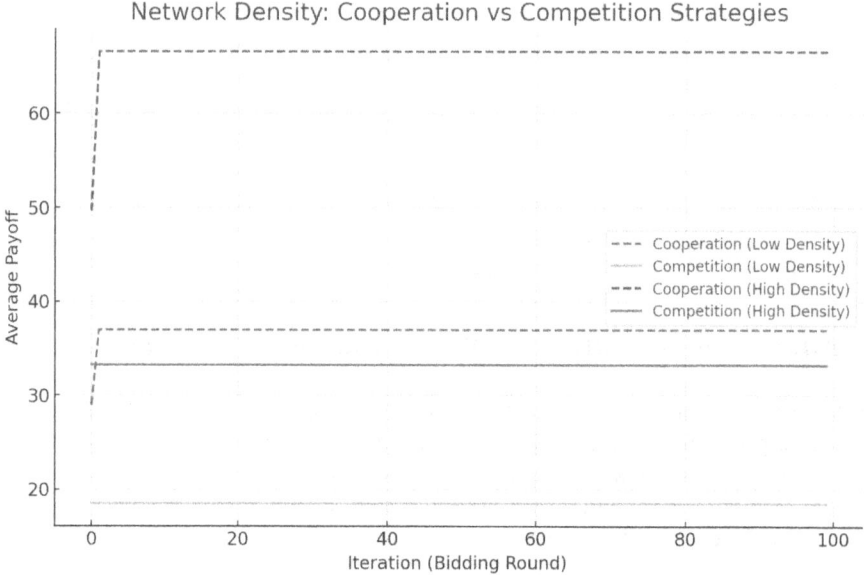

The simulation results show that when 60% of enterprises choose high-price strategies in the initial stage, enterprise earnings tend to stabilize more quickly. This suggests that in a situation where more companies choose to bid higher, it is easier for companies to reach stable bidding strategies, thereby reducing earnings fluctuations. In contrast, when only 40 percent of companies initially opt for a high-price strategy, the volatility of earnings is greater and companies need more rounds to find a balance point.

8 More Parametric Analysis Results

8.1 The Impact of Game Rounds

By extending the number of game rounds to 200, we observed that the returns of the cooperative strategy and the competitive strategy further tended to stabilize. Under the cooperative strategy, companies formed a relatively consistent strategy after multiple rounds of bidding, while the competitive strategy, due to frequent strategy adjustments, had more volatile returns. Although the final returns gradually stabilized, the overall level of returns was still lower than that of the cooperative strategy.

8.2 The Impact of Network Density

We also simulated the bidding behavior of enterprises under different cooperative network densities. In low-density networks, where there are fewer partnerships among enterprises, the revenue fluctuations of competitive strategies are particularly significant, and enterprises face more uncertainty when adjusting strategies. In contrast, in high-density networks, companies have achieved relatively stable returns through cooperative strategies, while competitive strategies, although more volatile at the beginning, tend to stabilize eventually.

9 Conclusion

This study shows that as cooperative networks evolve, the bidding strategies and results of enterprises are significantly influenced by the network structure. Enterprises with high degree centrality were able to dominate the bidding process, while those with high intermediate centrality and proximity centrality increased the success rate of bidding through information superiority. Future research could further optimize the model in combination with specific bidding data and apply 9. Parametric analysis and conclusions of network evolution.

In the bidding game of clean energy enterprises, the evolution of the network structure has a significant impact on the enterprise strategy and revenue. By analyzing the evolution of the network at different stages, we can find that network density, the distance between nodes, and the closeness of partnerships play a key role in the formation of the bidding strategy. Specifically, indicators such as Degree Centrality, Betweenness Centrality, and Closeness Centrality directly affect the position and role of enterprises in the bidding network.

9.1 Conclusions of the Parametric Analysis

1. In the case of high degree centrality, enterprises usually have more cooperation opportunities and can effectively integrate resources during the bidding process. High centrality enables these enterprises to dominate the market through extensive partnerships, thereby gaining more advantages in the bidding process.
2. Enterprises with a high degree of intermediary centrality play a crucial role in the transmission of information and can enhance their competitiveness in the bidding by acting as a bridge between partners. In this case, enterprises with high intermediary centrality can take advantage of the information asymmetry to form a strategic advantage in the bidding.
3. Companies with high proximity centrality are able to respond more quickly to market changes and adjustments to bidding strategies because of their shorter cooperation distance with other companies. This enables them to be more flexible in adjusting their bidding strategies in response to changes in the market and to achieve stable returns.

In summary, through parameter analysis of different stages of network evolution, we find that the complexity of the network structure has a profound impact on the formation of enterprise bidding strategies. Especially in a highly competitive market environment, enterprises that can occupy advantageous network positions tend to gain higher returns in the long-term game.

References

Jiang, X., Wang, P., Zhou, Y.: Complex network analysis of power bidding strategies. Energy Econ. **45**, 123–134 (2020)

Wang, T., Li, J., Chen, X.: Centrality measures in the analysis of bidding strategies in energy markets. Int. J. Energy Res. **43**(2), 457–469 (2019)

Zhang, M., Li, H.: Game theory applications in clean energy bidding: a review. Renewable Energy **65**, 89–99 (2021)

Li, Q., Zhou, M., He, Y.: Cooperation vs competition: a comparative study of energy companies' bidding strategies. J. Clean. Prod. **112**, 314–327 (2022)

Liu, S., Wang, X., Zhang, P.: Renewable energy incentives and their impact on energy market bidding. Energy Policy **70**, 244–253 (2020)

Ling, J., Ma, T., Chen, N., Liu, X., Gao, B.: A game theoretical approach based bidding strategy optimization for power producers in power markets with renewable electricity. Energies **10**(5), 627 (2017)

Xie, X., Ying, L., Cui, X.: Price strategy analysis of electricity retailers based on evolutionary game on complex networks. Sustainability **14**(15), 9487 (2022)

Guangxi Power Exchange Center Co., Ltd., & Hubei Engineering and Technology Research Center. Research on Renewable Energy Trading Strategies Based on Evolutionary Game Theory. Sustainability **16**(7), 2671 (2024)

Constructing the Data Factor Market Ecosystem: Pathways and Mechanisms

Hui Jiang(✉) , Dashan Liu, and Mengjiao Wang

Shandong Technology and Business University, Yantai, Shandong Province, China
`Jianghui0927@sdtbu.edu.cn`

Abstract. Employing an institutional-technical co-evolution lens, this study utilizes grounded theory research in YT City to uncover the multi-layered construction pathway of the data factor market ecosystem. Findings reveal that under the symbiotic effect of the institutional construction layer (policy momentum-driven) and the technical empowerment layer (infrastructure-supported), market entities realize factor value-added through the value emergence layer (business model innovation), while the dynamic stabilizer (governance adaptation) maintains system equilibrium. YT City's pioneering "Six-in-One" model demonstrates how typical prefecture-level cities can overcome data silos through institutional-technical inter-embedding, providing a novel paradigm for the data factor market in non-pilot cities nationwide.

Keywords: Data Factor Market Ecosystem · Institutional-Technical Symbiosis · Grounded Theory · Governance Adaptation

1 Introduction

1.1 Problem Statement

Achieving the data factor market is a key link in unlocking data value. In December 2022, the State Council issued the "Opinions on Building Foundational Data Systems to Better Leverage the Role of Data Factors" (commonly known as the "Data Twenty Articles"), establishing foundational data systems and encouraging the advancement of data sharing, opening, exchange, and trading focusing on key areas and scenarios such as intelligent manufacturing, energy conservation and carbon reduction, and smart cities [1], to realize the circulation and value of data factor. To fully leverage the multiplier effect of data factors, the National Data Administration, together with relevant departments, jointly issued the "Data Factor × Three-Year Action Plan (2024–2026)", proposing to concentrate on key industries and fields, mine high-value data factor application scenarios, promote the construction of data factor market ecosystem, realize their value and empower social development [2].

Within the framework of the above policy thinking, research on how to build the data factor market ecosystem is of practical significance [3]. However, the current data industry chain faces problems such as insufficient development of data resources, large stockpiles of "dark" or dormant data, and incomplete establishment of data security protection and infrastructure guarantee mechanisms [4], resulting in a "policy enthusiasm, implementation chill" dilemma in the data factor market. Existing research finds three patterns in data factor value-added practices across regions in China: mature leading, striving to catch up, and government-driven. The top-down developmental pattern has also become the primary model for regions with relatively backward big data industry development levels to carry out data factor value-added. A comprehensive understanding of the driving role and operational mechanism of application scenarios in the construction of the data element market ecosystem is needed to identify a sound and reliable ecological guarantee model [5].

This paper takes the non-pilot city YT City as a sample for case study, proposing the core question: How do institutions and technology collaboratively construct the path to the data factor market ecosystem?

1.2 Theoretical Perspective

Current domestic and international research on data factor market allocation and value-added mainly focuses on defining data factors, mechanisms and paths for data factor value-added, and data factor rights confirmation, lacking studies from the perspective of the data factor ecosystem. Drawing on the structural model of information ontology, information actors, and information environment from information ecology theory [6], the application scenario-driven data factor circulation ecosystem can be summarized as: within the legal, regulatory, and policy framework, based on service needs, governance needs, and future visions, mobilizing relevant actors to apply data products & services, and digital technologies to specific scenarios, ensuring scenario functionality realization and maximizing data value release.

Simultaneously, through data product & service innovation, iterative innovation of application scenarios is achieved [7]. It is a closed-loop system driven by application scenarios for the formation of the data value chain and continuous improvement of the related supporting environment [8]. Therefore, by examining how multiple relevant actors collaboratively realize data factor value through data authorization, trading, and

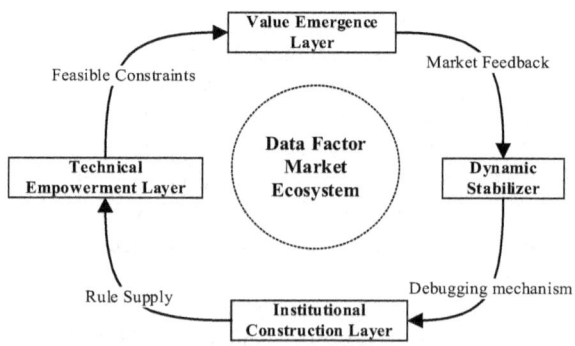

Fig. 1. Institutional-Technical Symbiosis Model of the Data Factor Market Ecosystem

circulation in the market construction process [9], analyzing the internal mechanisms of the data factor market, and further exploring the construction path, this paper proposes an institutional-technical symbiosis model from the perspective of information ecology theory, as shown in Fig. 1.

2 Research Methodology

2.1 Grounded Theory Design

This study adopts the procedural grounded theory method, using the three-level coding paradigm (open coding, axial coding, selective coding) as the core framework, combined with multi-source qualitative data on data factor market in YT City, to construct the "institutional-technical symbiotic market" theoretical model. The discussion unfolds from three aspects: methodological choice, design implementation, and methodological innovation.

Grounded theory is suitable for exploring the complex mechanisms of the emerging field of "data factor market". Its advantage lies in its theory-generating orientation, emphasizing the bottom-up generation of theory from raw data, avoiding interference from preset assumptions, and fitting the research needs of the "policy-technology-market" multiple interactions in the data factor market. Through theoretical sampling, the focus of data collection was dynamically adjusted (e.g., shifting from policy texts to enterprise interviews), responding to YT City's policy iteration process from "inventory table pilot" to "supply-demand matching," and clarifying the logical chain of institutional and technical variables [10].

2.2 Data Collection

Data collection and organization centered on the data factor market ecosystem, ensuring the reliability and validity of the research through triangulation of different data sources. There are three specific data sources: First, in-depth interviews. The research team obtained relevant materials through semi-structured interviews with staff of the Big Data Bureau and relevant enterprise management, as well as multiple interviews with board secretaries. Second, on-site observation. The research team observed the specific processes of digital factor market work by attending data supply-demand matching meetings and the Data Factor × competition. Third, secondary data. Adhering to the principle that "everything is data," the research team extensively collected secondary data such as policy documents (e.g., "YT City Public Data Authorization Operation Management Measures"), as well as related research papers, media reports, news interviews, and internal materials. Data collection details are shown in Table 1.

2.3 Data Coding

Open Coding. Open coding (Table 2) involves labeling collected data, summarizing label meanings to generate related concepts and categories at the next level, achieving layer-by-layer data refinement. Specifically: First, the research team screened statements in valid sample data involving data factors, enterprise data, data property rights, data monetization, data value, etc., and labeled them. Similar labels and related details were summarized until theoretical saturation of concepts was reached, forming 51 theory-related labels. Second, based on professional terminology, the team integrated and eliminated existing and new concepts extracted from literature and practical materials, resulting in 15 concepts. Finally, through repeated comparison and in-depth analysis of data, concepts, and categories, 9 categories were summarized.

Table 1. Data Types and Sources for Grounded Theory Research in YT City

Data Source	Source Example	Volume/Duration	Function Positioning
Policy Documents	YT City Public Data Authorization Operation Mgmt. Measures	32 documents	Analysis of Institutional Drivers
Semi-structured Interviews	Big Data Bureau staff, Corporate CEOs (12 persons)	441 min recording	Analysis of Value Emergence Behavior
Participatory Obs. Notes	Data Supply-Demand Matching Meetings (2023–2025)	18 sessions notes	Tracking Governance Adaptation
Corporate Archives	Corporate Annual Reports, Data Trading Contracts	17 enterprises	Verification of Tech. Empowerment Fit

Axial Coding. This paper formed the main categories required for coding by arranging, combining, refining, and eliminating the obtained categories. Simultaneously, by placing categories into the "causal conditions-phenomenon-action strategies-outcome" causal relationship analysis model, the logical relationships between categories were identified. The interpretation and connotation of axial coding are shown in Table 3.

Selective Coding. Selective coding involves further inductive analysis of the obtained data and hierarchical categories. Through continuous process deduction and rationalized connections between categories, the highest-level core category is identified. Then, based on the full interaction between theory and data, a complete theoretical framework and category interpretation method is derived. This paper further condensed the four main categories "Institutional Empowerment," "Technical Constraints," "Market Emergence," and "Governance Adaptation" to form the core category "Institutional-Technical Symbiosis of the Data Factor market Ecosystem."

Table 2. Example of Open Coding

Label	Concept	Category
a1 State proposes data factor concept (coordinating data property rights, circulation/trading, etc.)		
a2 Issuance of Government Data Sharing Regulations	A1 Market Allocation of Data Factors	
a3 Implementation of Data Factor × Action Plan	A2 Breaking Departmental Data Silos	
a4 Implementation of Public Data Authorization Operation Registration Mgmt. Measures	A3 Public Data Asset Management	C1 Political Momentum
a5 Promotion of Enterprise Data Asset Inventory Table Mgmt. Measures	A4 Exploration of Data Asset Financialization	C2 Institutional Rigidity
……	A5 Incentivizing Enterprise Data Resource Development	C3 Ambiguous Ownership
a10 Unclear Data Property Rights	A6 Rights Confirmation Difficulties Hinder market	C4 Infrastructure
a12 High AI Model Dev. Cost for SMEs (Requiring 2–3 Million RMB Investment)	A7 Computing Power & Data Silos Constrain Application	C5 Economic Incentive
a13 Data Dev. Group Receives Bank Credit (CEB 3M/Qilu Bank 15M RMB)	A8 Exploration of Data Asset Financialization	C6 Demand Traction
……	A9 Data-Driven Financial Innovation	C7 Technology Enhancement
a30 GT Group Achieves Pure Data Product Mortgage Loan	A10 Enhancing Data Usability	C8 Privacy Monetization
a31 DE Shares & 10 Other Enterprises Apply for High-Quality Datasets	A11 Discovering Enterprise Data Utilization Needs	C9 Knowledge Extraction
a32 Conducting Data Factor Supply-Demand Matching Activities	A12 Incentive's Data Resource Opening	
a33 Application of Data Annotation Technology	A13 Data Directly Generating Commercial Value	
a34 Consumer Behavior Data Collection	A14 Data Monopoly Deriving New Services	

(*continued*)

Table 2. (*continued*)

Label	Concept	Category
......	A15 Industrial Data Knowledge Monetization	
a50 Mandatory Use of Tobacco Payment Tools		
a51 Chemical Process Data Sedimentation		

Table 3. Interpretation and Connotation of Axial Coding

Main Category	Category	Interpretation
Institutional Empowerment	C1 Political Momentum	National-level promotion of data factor market allocation
	C2 Institutional Rigidity	Issuance of Government Data Sharing Regulations
Technical Constraints	C3 Ambiguous Ownership	Unclear data property rights
	C4 Infrastructure	Lack of trusted data space
Value Emergence	C5 Economic Incentive	Policies encouraging high-quality dataset applications
	C6 Demand Traction	Discovering enterprise data needs
Governance Adaptation	C7 Technology Enhancement	Enhancement of related technologies like data annotation
	C8 Privacy Monetization	Capability for anonymized consumer data analysis
	C9 Knowledge Extraction	Production process optimization diagnostic services

3 Findings and Discussion

3.1 Driving Mechanism of the Institutional Construction Layer

YT City achieved "breakthrough as a non-pilot city" through policy nested design. Vertical nesting: Transforming the national "Data Twenty Articles" into local registration management measures. Horizontal nesting: Jointly formulating asset inventory table processes with the Finance Bureau to resolve the contradiction between the public welfare nature and market of public data.

"We worked with the Finance Bureau in a closed loop, with proceeds entering the treasury for redistribution" (Interview ID YT2025-P03)

A "Big Data Bureau (decision-making) - Data Development Group (operation) - Research Institute (evaluation)" iron triangle structure was established, realizing the governance innovation of "separation of regulation and operation." In the data asset inventory table process, requirements from the "Enterprise Accounting Standards" and "Cybersecurity Law" were synchronously embedded, establishing a compliance review firewall (Interview YT2025-F01). Breaking the simple imitation logic of institutional transplantation theory (Dolowitz, 2000), it reveals that institutional nested design (Institutional Embedding) is key to cracking "policy suspension".

3.2 Adaptive Innovation in the Technical Empowerment Layer

The core of technical empowerment in YT City's practice exhibits distinct characteristics of progressive adaptation. Its innovation logic lies in achieving dynamic coupling between technical capabilities and the institutional environment through infrastructure iteration.

According to YT City's practical exploration, its data infrastructure evolution follows the path dependence law in the social construction of technology, specifically manifested in three leaps.

Collection-Oriented 1.0 Stage (2019–2021). Built an integrated big data platform to solve the physical centralization of government data, but faced institutional inertia of data silos. Technology at this stage acted as a tool for executing administrative orders, reflecting the passive attribute of technological instrumentalism.

Integration-Oriented 2.0 Stage (2022–2023). Established a securities supervision comprehensive data platform, generating grassroots governance applications (e.g., medical insurance fraud screening) by integrating ministry data with local foundational databases. This stage validated technological intermediation theory, where technology acts as a solvent for departmental barriers, but was limited by ambiguous data ownership.

Trust-Oriented 3.0 Stage (2024-). Planning a trusted data space, introducing privacy-preserving computation technology to achieve "usable but invisible" government-enterprise data. In the satellite image data annotation case, agricultural experts used annotation tools to correct CNN algorithm segmentation errors, forming a human-machine collaborative knowledge production cycle, powerfully refuting the myth of technological determinism. This process profoundly illustrates critical technical theory—annotation technology is neither a pure tool (constrained by expert cognition) nor an autonomous system (requiring institutional guarantees for data quality), but a product jointly constructed by institutional norms, market demands, and agricultural knowledge.

3.3 Localized Innovation in the Value Emergence Layer

The value emergence layer is the product of the adaptive behavior of market entities during the data factor market process. Its innovative essence lies in realizing data value through localization strategies. Distinct from the mandatory change of top-level institutional design, this layer exhibits distinct demand-induced characteristics, specifically manifested as value creation model innovation and market self-organization evolution.

Three Types of Value Creation Models

Resource Reorganization: Releasing asset value through data rights confirmation.

For example, the bus group reorganized passenger flow data into "Passenger Flow Heatmap Spectrum." After data asset valuation, it obtained a 15 million RMB credit line from Qilu Bank, achieving the leap from resource accumulation to capital transformation. This established a "data asset-financial credit" mapping channel, solving the dilemma of non-physical asset mortgages, and innovating the data value creation model.

Knowledge Encapsulation: Realizing data value by converting tacit knowledge into explicit knowledge.

GG Intelligence encoded chemical experts' process experience into algorithm parameters, forming a reusable large model for reaction process optimization, and outputting explicit industrial knowledge to small and medium-sized chemical enterprises through SaaS subscription services.

Risk Prevention & Control: Transforming consumption data into risk supervision measurement tools.

The tobacco company captured anonymous consumption data through payment terminals, building an "Abnormal Purchase Identification Model." This achieved precision marketing (reducing customer acquisition costs) while enhancing law enforcement efficiency (shortening case tracing cycles).

Market Self-organization Characteristics

Data Demand Side: Enterprises proactively raised the demand for "Data Property Rights Certificates."

Increased data transaction frequency spurred rights confirmation needs; asset mortgage scenarios required proof of ownership; judicial rights protection needed legal basis. Portlink Group achieved pure data product mortgages, demonstrating market entities' potential to realize data factor value.

Data Supply Side: Consumption platforms formed knowledge aggregation evolution by analyzing high-value datasets.

The data supply side dynamically optimized data collection dimensions. Merchants independently accessed the system, making the dataset value far exceed the sum of single-point data. For example, Weicheng Zhijia spontaneously formed a dataset from 30,000 merchants, creating a consumer behavior knowledge graph, fully realizing data factor value.

Overall, the data value emergence layer exhibits a co-evolution characteristic of "Institutional Demand - Knowledge supply."

3.4 Regulatory Role of the Dynamic Stabilizer

The dynamic stabilizer functions as an adaptive governance hub in YT City's data factor market. Its essence is the process where multiple actors promote institutional iteration through policy learning. This study identified three significant governance shifts, revealing the symbiotic evolution path of "policy cognition - action strategy - institutional evolution" (Table 4).

"Only when all roads were blocked did we understand: the core of data factor market is supply and demand." (Memo YT2025-M12).

Table 4. Three Stages of Policy Governance Shift

Stage	Dominant Coalition	Core Belief	Key Action	Institutional Consequence
Norm Reinforcement Period (2023)	Finance-Audit Coalition	Rule Centrism (Confirm Rights Before Circulation)	Implemented Data Asset Inventory Pilot	Faced enterprise resistance to rights confirmation (86% feedback unfeasible)
Flexible Adjustment Period (2024)	Big Data-Enterprise Coalition	Demand Orientation (Promote Circulation Through Use)	Conducted Supply-Demand Matching for 50 Enterprises	Spurred innovative cases like Portlink Data Mortgage
Ecosystem Cultivation Period (2025)	Gov-Industry-Academia-Research Coalition	System Symbiosis (Factor × Ecosystem)	Built Data Factor × Ecosystem	Formed Institutional-Technology-Market Triangular Cycle

4 Research Summary

This study constructs a multi-level theoretical framework for data factor market through the three-level coding of grounded theory. Its core value lies in bridging the gap between policy discourse and technical practice, providing a replicable market path for non-pilot areas. It is the first to apply grounded theory to prefecture-level city data factor market research, building a three-level coding system, proposing an "institutional-technical symbiotic market" model. It breaks through the "policy-market" dualistic framework, revealing the mutual construction relationship between policy regulation (institutional construction core) and technical capability (technical empowerment core), overcoming the dualism of new institutional economics and technological determinism. Practically, it also has innovation, breakthroughly summarizing the "Six-in-One" data market path for non-pilot areas, providing practical reference for prefecture-level cities nationwide.

Acknowledgements. This article acknowledges funding by Natural Science Foundation Project of Shandong Province (grant number ZR2022MG074).

Disclosure of Interests. The authors have no competing interests to declare that are relevant to the content of this article.

References

1. Yin, X.M., Chen, J., Wang, G.: Scenario-driven: a new mechanism of market-oriented allocation of data elements for new productivity. Soc. Sci. J. **2**(3), 178–188 (2024)
2. Ye Yongwei, Y., Tiantian, T.Y., et al.: The stable investment effect of government data element sharing: evidence from public data open platforms. J. Quant. Tech. Econ. **42**(01), 136–156 (2025)

3. Chen, L., Li, M.Z., Xue, Q.Y.: Realistic constraints and path selection of data element market construction. Reform **2**(1), 83–94 (2023)
4. Jin, X.H., Tan, X., Li, H.: Enabling the development of the real economy through the multiplier effect of data elements: mechanism and path selection. Inf. Stud. Theory Appl. **47**(6), 31–38 (2024)
5. Gu, J., Liu, Y.B., Wang, Z., et al.: Assessment of urban data element market readiness from the perspective of information ecology theory. J. Inf. Resour. Manag. **14**(2), 82–94 (2024)
6. Botao, D.: Research on the data element market based on information ecology theory. Theory Pract. Inf. Sci. **59**(12), 36–41 (2022)
7. Ding, B.T., Chen, C., Gao, F., et al.: Experts' opinions: the impact of the establishment of the National Data Bureau on the future of big data. Documentation Inf. Knowl. **40**(3), 13–24 (2023)
8. Wu, W.Q., Li, Q.H., Zhang, L.Y., et al.: Public data resources and enterprise total factor productivity: a quasi-natural experiment based on local government data opening. Syst. Eng. Theory Pract. **44**(6), 1815–1833 (2024)
9. Zhu, H.Y.: The current situation and countermeasures of data trading platforms from the perspective of data elements circulation. China Bus. Market **38**(2), 24–33 (2024)
10. Chunlong, Z., Haiqun, M., Jin, W.: Research on the model and path of public data value release from the perspective of ecosystem. Libr. Inf. Serv. **69**(03), 3–13 (2025)

Exploring the Construction of Training Communities: A Case Study of the Smart City Management Technology Major

Zhu Xiangbo[✉]

School of Construction Engineering, Shenzhen Polytechnic University, Shenzhen 518055, Guangdong, China
zxb@szpt.edu.cn

Abstract. China's vocational education system has undergone profound institutional changes guided by policies. Since 2019, the revision of the Vocational Education Law of the People's Republic of China and the introduction of a series of policy documents such as the Implementation Plan for National Vocational Education Reform, have marked the formal establishment of vocational education as a "type of education" and valued alongside general education. In this context, the pilot implementation of the "Vocational College Entrance Examination" system and the establishment of vocational undergraduate colleges have further strengthened the cultivation path of technical and skilled talents. In 2021, "Ministry of Education of the People's Republic of China" issued the "Catalogue of Vocational Education Specialties (2021)", "which newly added the major of "smart city management technology" and categorized under the category of civil engineering and construction" "smart city management technology" was added, which is categorized under the category of civil engineering and construction. The establishment of this specialty is in line with the national strategic demand for the integration of new urbanization and digitalization, and aims to cultivate compound technical and skilled talents with the ability of planning, construction, operation and management of smart cities. Based on the Professional Teaching Standards for Vocational Education, this paper discusses the construction and operation of the practical training community by combining the practical training practices of some typical colleges and universities.

Keywords: Training Community · Smart City Management Technology Major · Construction Model

1 Introduction

In recent years, China's vocational education system has realized systematic changes and high-quality development under the guidance of policies. The National Conference on Vocational Education held in April 2021 was of landmark significance, in which General Secretary Xi Jinping explicitly pointed out, "Accelerate the construction of a modern vocational education system, and cultivate more high-quality technical and skilled talents, skilled craftsmen, and great national craftsmen ", this important instruction pointed out the direction for the development of vocational education in the new era and established the strategic position of vocational education (Xinhua News Agency, 2021) [1].

At the policy level, the newly revised Vocational Education Law of the People's Republic of China in 2022 clearly stipulates at the legal level that "vocational education is a type of education that has the same importance as general education" and defines in detail the connotations and objectives of vocational education (Standing Committee of the National People's Congress, 2022) [2]. The law innovatively puts forward the positioning of enterprises as an important school-running body, and requires enterprises to deeply participate in the whole process of vocational education, including key links such as specialty setting, textbook development, and cultivation program development.

At the practical level, the hierarchical structure of vocational education in China continues to be optimized. Since the launch of the undergraduate-level vocational education pilot program in 2019, vocational undergraduate education has developed rapidly. According to data from the Ministry of Education, as of May 2025, there are 83 undergraduate-level vocational colleges (universities), with 298 higher-level undergraduate majors and a planned enrollment of 550,000 students. This development trend fully reflects China's determination and effectiveness in building a modern vocational education system.

Smart city, as an advanced form of urban development, utilizes new-generation information technologies such as Internet of Things, cloud computing, big data, spatial geographic information, etc., to promote intelligent urban planning, construction, management and services. Smart city can be subdivided into many dimensions such as smart industry, smart governance, smart environment and smart life. Smart city involves a wide range of aspects and applications, and smart city management has high requirements for intelligence, digitization and informatization.

In 2021, the specialty of smart city management technology was entered into the higher vocational education specialties of the Ministry of Education, belonging to the category of urban and rural planning and management (category code: 4402) under the major category of civil engineering and construction (major code :44), which is mainly oriented to the development of the smart city and the construction of the digital city to cultivate specialized talents. The construction of the specialty must follow the direction of the development of vocational education in the new era, especially in practical training and teaching to fully reflect the characteristics of industry-teaching integration and school-enterprise cooperation. At present, the construction of the specialty faces such key issues as how to transform policy requirements into effective practice and how to build a practical training system adapted to the needs of the development of the smart city industry, which urgently requires in-depth research and practical exploration.

2 Literature Review

As the core link of vocational education talent training, the quality of practical training directly determines the cultivation effectiveness of skilled talents (Ding Ji'an, 2004) [3]. Comparative research shows that developed countries have formed their own distinctive practical training and teaching models. Such as, Germany's "dual system" realizes the integration of theory and practice through the engineering alternation mechanism of school-enterprise collaboration. The American CBE model is guided by competency standards to build a modular curriculum system. The UK NVQ system relies on vocational qualifications to achieve standardized assessment of learning outcomes (OECD, 2019) [4, 5]. Together, these models highlight the key role of work process systematization in practical training and teaching.

Researches showed the integration model of industry and education is evolving from a single cooperation to a systematic collaboration. Declan (2017) divides it into three basic modes from the perspective of actors: teaching cooperation, research cooperation and multiple integration [6]. Li Dan (2018) put forward the concept of "community of interests" from the perspective of organizational form, emphasizing the sharing mechanism of resources and interests [7]. With the deepening of research, Zheng Yanqiu (2019) innovatively proposed the "community" model of "government-school-enterprise" tripartite collaboration, revealing the coupling relationship between regional economic development and talent training [8]. Fang Yiquan (2020) further developed the theoretical framework of "a community with a shared future for the integration of industry and education", and systematically constructed a multi-agent collaborative ecosystem based on a common vision [9].

In addition, some research focus on the operation mechanism and influencing factors of industry-education integration community. Harald Knudsen (2015) research shows that the conditions of vocational colleges and universities (including professional settings, teacher level and organizational execution, etc.) are the key endogenous factors [10]. In terms of model innovation, Zhu Yanfeng (2020) proposed the "Five Together" (school-enterprise co-innovation, specialty co-construction, talent co-cultivation, team co-growth, and resource co-enjoyment) collaborative education model based on the practice of industrial colleges, which systematically explains the operation mechanism of school-enterprise cooperation [11]. Zou Yuxiang (2021) constructed the theoretical framework of "double helix", which deepened the operation theory of the integration of industry and education through the interaction between the external helix system of "government-institution-enterprise" and the internal helix system of "knowledge-skill-quality" [12].

While some researchers put forward the concept of "training community", Wu Zhi (2018) proposed that the essence of community is the in-depth interaction of multiple subjects based on complementary advantages [13]. Peng Xue (2020) further pointed out that its core characteristics include goal consistency, member heterogeneity, and action synergy [14]. In terms of practical dilemmas, Zhan Huashan (2020) found that there are three obstacles: institutional absence, mismatch between supply and demand, and resource imbalance [15]. Chen Zhijie (2021) emphasized that the lack of certification system makes it difficult to form a demonstration effect. These studies provide a theoretical basis for understanding the supposed and actual state of the industry-education integration community, but they still need to be deepened in terms of institutional innovation path and dynamic adjustment mechanism [16].

Some scholars have conducted practical applications and research on the "practical training community." Jin Enmao (2025) introduced a construction plan for a smart city management technology practical training laboratory. In terms of practical training modules, technologies such as BIM, IoT, sensors, and data analysis are employed, covering modules such as building comprehensive cabling, security control, and smart home systems, and encompassing scenarios such as building intelligent management, park intelligent management, and smart city management [17]. Cai Qingqing, Fu Bin, Wang Jian, et al. (2024) explored professional practice teaching based on VR/AR, pointing out that VR/AR practical teaching faces issues such as unstable software environments, inconsistent hardware quality, insufficient teaching resources, and inadequate research support teams. They proposed the construction of a virtual simulation practical training base co-built by government, schools, industries, and enterprises to conduct virtual-combined practical teaching [18].

In general, the existing research on the integration of practical training and teaching and industry and education has been very comprehensive. In the stage of the evolution of the industry-education integration model to the 'community', further research on the operational mode and dynamic mechanism is conducted at the theoretical level, and the application research of emerging subjects in the context of digital transformation is carried out at the practical level.

3 Development and Requirements of Smart City Management Technology Major

3.1 Phased Characteristics

In 2021, the Ministry of Education's Higher Vocational Education Specialty Catalogue set up the smart city management technology major, and as of 2025, a total of 36 universities across the country has already offer this major. From the perspective of overall development, it mainly has the following characteristics:

First, balanced regional distribution: covering the multi-province school-running pattern from economically developed areas in the east (Beijing, Shanghai, Guangdong and Zhejiang) to underdeveloped provinces in the west (Yunnan, Guizhou, Gansu and Guizhou), mainly relying on urban or construction vocational colleges. Second, the differentiation of professional origins: one category is the transformation of civil engineering, mainly from "real estate operation and management" and "property management" and other majors, focusing on "management technology". The other is urban transformation, which mainly comes from the upgrading of "urban management" and "information management", highlighting "digital technology". Third, cultivate positioning compounding: focus on the needs of new urbanization, build a dual-core capability system of "digital technology urban management", and focus on cultivating intelligent operation and maintenance capabilities such as BIM/CIM applications and digital twin modeling.

3.2 Basic Requirements

In March 2025, the Ministry of Education's "Teaching Standards for Smart City Management Technology Majors in Higher Vocational Education" was released, which comprehensively and meticulously stipulates the training objectives, core courses and practical training requirements.

First, Talent Training Goals. Majoring in civil engineering, professional technical services and public facilities management and other industries, it cultivates talents with urban information system integration, data collection and analysis, intelligent facility operation and maintenance and urban comprehensive management, and can engage in urban information model modelling and application photogrammetry and remote sensing, geographic information system application, municipal infrastructure management, urban community management, smart city operation and governance, etc.

Second, the Professional Core Curriculum System. To support the cultivation of the professional ability of students, the following fields of courses need to be set up. Fields and main teaching content of the curriculum system are shown in Table 1 below:

Third, the Professional Training Curriculum System. The mainly completes practical training through classroom experiments, internship training and graduation projects. In terms of practical training, it covers urban information modelling (CIM) modelling, UAV flight control and maintenance, GIS software application, etc., while through the forms like individual skill training, comprehensive ability training, productive training. In terms of internship, professional internships are carried out in civil engineering and construction, professional technical services and public facilities management and other industries, including understanding internship and job internship, and completing the graduation project. The tasks and equipment requirements required for practical training are shown in Table 2 below:

4 Construction Practice of Smart City Management Technology Major in Typical Universities

The smart city management technology major is a typical interdisciplinary field, involving advanced technologies such as the Internet of Things, big data, artificial intelligence, cloud computing, digital twins, and geographic information. In the construction of training resources, it is essential to cover these key technologies as much as possible to ensure that students' skills can meet industry demands..

In the field of higher vocational education evaluation in China, the "China University and Discipline Evaluation Report" published by the China Academy for Science and Education Evaluation (CASEE) is widely recognized. In the rankings for the Smart City Management Technology major from 2021 to 2025, institutions such as Zhejiang University of Construction, Wuhan Technical University, Shenzhen Polytechnic University, and Shandong Urban Construction Vocational College have consistently ranked among the top (almost always in the top five). Additionally, these institutions were among the first in China to establish smart city management technology programs. Some originated from management-related programs such as "urban management," others from architecture-related programs like "real estate operations and management," and some from information technology-related programs such as "urban digitization." Consequently, these institutions have developed distinct approaches to program construction and practical training, resulting in notable characteristics in talent cultivation. Conducting related analyses of these institutions holds significant typological value.

Table 1. The fields and main teaching content of the curriculum system

Course Areas	Typical job description	Main teaching content
City Information Modelling (CIM) Technology and Applications	Creation and visualization of urban information models, and specific applications of urban management	Modelling technology, visualization technology and integrated application technology of urban information model
Photogrammetry and remote sensing technology	Urban spatial data collection, data element extraction, and spatiotemporal information analysis	Basic technology of remote sensing, UAV measurement technology, spatio-temporal data analysis technology
Geographic Information System (GIS) Technology and Applications	Establishment of geographic information database, data modelling, database maintenance and management	Basic knowledge of geographic information systems, knowledge of spatial data collection and management, software use and application
Municipal infrastructure planning and management	Municipal infrastructure data collection, municipal infrastructure operation and maintenance and management	Basic knowledge of urban infrastructure, operation and maintenance, construction and management technology of various infrastructures
Urban community construction and management	Urban community grid management, social service management, community organization and management	Basic knowledge of urban community management and services, modern urban community construction and management methods and technologies
Smart city operations and governance	Urban management data collection and processing, smart city information management platform construction and maintenance	Basic knowledge of smart city operation and governance, design, construction technology and application technology of smart city information management platform

4.1 The Practice of Wuhan Technical University

Wuhan Technical University (WTU) is one of the first colleges in China to offer smart city management technology majors, and its development path is "digital city-urban information management-smart city management technology", forming a dual-core training system of "urban construction information management", focusing on the construction of smart city platform and application ability training. In 2024, the first batch of graduates are mainly engaged in BIM engineers and modelling engineers. The positions for talents mainly include core job groups such as "urban grid member", "modelling engineer"

Table 2. The tasks and equipment requirements required for practical training

Practical training field	Main training tasks	Main equipment requirements:
Practical training of basic skills	Architectural drawings and drawings	Architectural drawing, drawing and drafting equipment and software
Geographic information surveying and mapping training	UAV flight control and maintenance	Level, theodolite, total station, 3D laser scanner, navigation and positioning system, drone
Urban information modelling and application training	Building Information Modelling (BIM), Urban Information Modelling (CIM), 3D Modelling	Computer-aided design, graphic image processing, real-life 3D modelling, simulation platform
Geographic Information System (GIS) training	photogrammetry and remote sensing, geographic information system (GIS) technology application	photogrammetry and remote sensing technology, geographic information system (GIS) technology and applications

and "geographic information engineer", as well as emerging technology positions such as "surveying and mapping engineer" and "drone pilot". To ensure the pertinence and quality of talent training, vocational skill level certificates such as building information modelling (BIM), digital twin city modelling and application, and smart community integration and operation and maintenance have been set up. In the practical training course, there are training rooms for architectural model making, drone flight, and oblique photogrammetry, and practical training such as smart city data collection, oblique photography, digital model production and data production. On the training base, it is jointly built and shared with Wuhan University Science and Technology Park and Huazhong University of Science and Technology Science Park to realize the whole process of "data collection, modelling, and application".

4.2 The Practice of Zhejiang University of Construction

Zhejiang University of Construction is the earliest college in China to offer smart city management technology majors, and the enrollment category is computer. Its origin originated from the establishment of the "Urban Information Management" major in 2011, and later set up the characteristic direction of "Digital Urban Management". Professionally cultivate "smart urban management" talents who are proficient in law enforcement practice and information technology, and can engage in urban modeling, data collection and analysis, intelligent detection and operation and maintenance of urban facilities. The positions are mainly "smart city management assistant", "data acquisition engineer", "system operation and maintenance engineer" and "data analyst". Skill certificates include smart city management certificates, secretary qualification certificates, ITAT educational engineering vocational qualification certificates and other certificates. In terms of training facilities, there is a smart urban management training center in the school to carry out digital urban management training. Outside the school, it has jointly built a training base with government agencies such as the Shaoxing Municipal Comprehensive Administrative Law Enforcement Bureau and the Quzhou Digital Urban Management Platform.

4.3 The Practice of Shandong Urban Construction Vocational College

In 2022, the "Real Estate Operation and Management" major transferred to the "Smart City Management Technology" major. Focus on smart city operation and governance, and cultivate high-skilled talents in the fields of urban information modelling (CIM) modelling, photogrammetry, GIS applications, and municipal facility management. It is mainly for civil engineering, surveying and mapping geographic information, public facilities management, software and information technology services and other industries, covering construction engineering technicians, surveying and mapping engineers, GIS application specialists, smart city operation specialists, community management services and other occupations. Skill certificates include digital twin city modelling and application, smart community integration and operation and maintenance and other certificates. In terms of practical training courses, the school has built a smart city training room and a digital twin training room (CIM modelling, VR virtual reality, etc.). On the off-campus training base, it is connected to the "Smart Housing and Construction Platform" of the Shandong Provincial Department of Housing and Urban-Rural Development, and links the CIM platforms of various cities to create a digital twin city practice system.

4.4 The Practice of Shenzhen Polytechnic University

In 2023, the smart city management technology major transferred from the original "real estate operation and management" major. Focus on urban management, urban renewal and real estate valuation, smart community management, and cultivate compound technical and skilled talents. In terms of positions, urban assets and facilities operation and maintenance, urban renewal and valuation, smart community (park) area management and other positions. The skill certificate includes Building Information Modeling (BIM), smart community integration and operation and maintenance, real estate data collection and database construction, etc. In terms of practical training equipment, it is equipped with a smart city big data center, a smart community management training center and a geographic information system training center. On the training platform, a training base has been jointly built with Shenzhen Anju Group, Shenzhen Smart City Technology, and Shenzhen Nanshan District Urban Big Data Centre.

4.5 Summary of Practical Training Teaching in these Schools

It can be seen from the practical training and teaching of the above-mentioned colleges and universities that the practical training and teaching content of smart city management technology major is complex and has high technical requirements. The design of the training content of each college cannot fully meet the needs of enterprises. The attempts of some colleges and universities have introduced government platforms, enterprise facilities, and industry certificates, and have achieved remarkable results.

While the Dilemmas faced by practical training teaching should also pay in-depth attention, during the practical process in various schools, it has been found that the smart city management technology training faces the following issues:

(1) **Wide professional coverage and high degree of technical integration**. The construction of smart cities involves cutting-edge technologies such as the Internet of Things, big data, digital twins, and cloud computing. At the same time, smart cities can be divided into multiple fields such as smart communities, smart transportation, smart government affairs, and smart environments.

(2) **Virtual simulation is difficult, and the authenticity of the training scene is insufficient.** The operation of the smart city management system requires a large amount of data resources. Real city data is sensitive and often not available to universities. At the same time, simple software simulation cannot replace the real city management scenario.

(3) **The equipment is updated quickly and the maintenance cost is high**. The various equipment for smart city management training, such as IoT sensors, AI servers, and digital twin workstations, are often expensive and can be replaced quickly. At the same time, the pertinence of talent training in different schools is inconsistent, and the models and types required may be more complex.

(4) **Teachers have high ability requirements and difficulty in integrating the curriculum system.** The application field of smart city requires the integration of multidisciplinary knowledge such as computer, urban planning, and public management, which school teachers often cannot master. At the same time, facing the multi-dimensional requirements of talent training and the complexity of positions, the curriculum system of smart city management technology major presents obvious complexity, which may require teachers from different majors to collaborate in teaching.

5 Path of Building a Practical Training Community

In October 2021, the General Office of the CPC Central Committee and the General Office of the State Council issued the Opinions on Promoting the High-Quality Development of Modern Vocational Education, which systematically put forward requirements such as "cooperation between schools and social capital in the construction of training bases", "vocational schools setting up internship training bases in enterprises and enterprises building training bases in vocational schools". The Opinions on the High-Quality Development of Schools and Social Capital Cooperation to Build Training Bases It promotes multi-party cooperation among the government, institutions, industries and enterprises, improves the comprehensive education mechanism of "post-course, race and certificate", designs and develops curricula in accordance with the actual production and job requirements of enterprises, and develops a modularized and systematic system of practical training curricula, so as to enhance the practical abilities of students.

5.1 The Formation of "Practical Training Community"

Intelligent city management technology involves "government, school, industry, enterprise, research" and other parties, and the collaboration of all parties to build "practical training community" is the key to improve the quality of talent training. Collaboration among all parties to build a "practical training community" is the key to improve the quality of talent training. Through the integration of resources and complementary advantages, we can realize the common construction of practical training environment, sharing of teachers, common research projects and common cultivation of talents.

Table 3. Components of a community of practice

Subjects	Roles	Contributions
Government (G)	Policy support, data openness, project guidance	Provide real data on smart cities, publish urban governance requirements, and provide financial subsidies or tax incentives
University (U)	Talent training, curriculum development, practical training management	Provide venues, infrastructural equipment and teaching teams; design a curriculum that meets industry standards; organize students to participate in real projects
Enterprise (E)	Technology empowerment, job matching, equipment support	Donating or leasing state-of-the-art equipment, providing engineers as adjunct faculty, opening internships
Associations (A)	Standard setting, resource coordination, certification assessment	Issuance of vocational skills standards, organization of industry competitions, promotion of "1 + X" certificates
Research Institutions	Technology research and development, transformation of results	Joint submission of projects and provision of training in cutting-edge technologies

5.2 The Cooperation Model of the Community

The cooperation model of the practical training community is constructed from the aspects of building practical training bases together, researching practical training programs together, sharing teachers and curricula, as well as jointly promoting certification and employment.

First, to jointly build practical training bases. Try to take the institution as the main body, multi-party participation in the construction of "smart city operation simulation center", the government provides real city management data, enterprises provide the corresponding algorithms and hardware equipment. Based on the training base, carry out practical training teaching, talent training and scientific research and development.

Second, co-development of practical training programs. Taking enterprises as the main body, adopt the joint development method of "teachers of institutions + engineers of enterprises" to implement the technology research and development related to smart cities and smart parks. In this process, the institutions and schools can participate in the basic research and preliminary design of the program.

Third, sharing teachers and courses. Institutions and enterprises as a common subject, enterprise engineering regularly resides in schools to teach courses related to the practice of smart city. Teachers from the university regularly go to the enterprises to participate in various projects of smart city.

Fourth, co-promote certification and employment. Taking the industry as the main body, relying on schools and enterprises, develop relevant vocational qualification certificates, which are incorporated into the credit system and graduation qualifications, and industry enterprises give priority to employing students who have passed the certificate authentication.

5.3 Operational System of the Community

First, the design of the organizational structure. The leading organization consists of government representatives, institutional leaders and enterprise executives, and is responsible for strategic decision-making. The executive body is implemented by the Academic Affairs Office of the institution, the HR department of the enterprise, and the secretariat of the industry association.

Second, resource integration mechanism. In terms of data resources, the government develops desensitized data, and enterprises provide cloud platform arithmetic. In terms of equipment resources, the enterprise equipment adopts the "rent + iteration" approach.

Third, benefit distribution mechanism. From the government's point of view, it will enhance the level of urban intelligence and cultivate localized technical talents. From the perspective of institutions, access to equipment, projects, employment resources. From the perspective of enterprises, prioritize the recruitment of talents and the transformation of joint R&D results.

Fourth, dynamic evaluation mechanism. Evaluate the operation status of the community according to the year, focusing on the completion of practical training programs, the rate of student employment counterparts, and enterprise satisfaction. Based on the evaluation results, optimization and adjustment will be carried out.

5.4 Implementation Points

First, clarify the rights and responsibilities of all parties. Sign the Community Cooperation Agreement, stipulating the terms of data security, intellectual property rights, and equipment maintenance. Second, create benchmark projects. Select 1 ~ 2 highly visible projects, quickly land and publicize them. Third, establish long-term communication. Hold monthly online joint meetings and organize quarterly offline technical discussions. Fourth, protect students' rights and interests. Enterprise projects need to clarify the scope of student participation and pay internship subsidies. Fifth, policy and financial support. The local government gives special support to the project and tax breaks to participating enterprises.

6 Conclusion

The core of the professional training community of intelligent city technology management is "complementary resources, benefit sharing and responsibility sharing". The government should provide timely policy dividends to promote the deep binding of schools and enterprises. Enterprises should be deeply involved in curriculum development and scientific research cooperation from the perspective of equipment and resource provision. Institutions should take the initiative to adapt, adjust talent training programs in a timely manner, and cooperate with the technology iteration of enterprises and industries. At the same time, the effectiveness of cooperation should be assessed regularly to avoid the community from becoming a mere formality. Through the construction of the community, it can effectively solve the pain points of insufficient practical training resources, lagging teaching content, poor employment docking, etc., and realize the integration of the three chains of "education chain-industry chain-innovation chain".

Acknowledgements. This research was supported by Ministry of Education Humanities and Social Science Research Youth Foundation (No. 19YJC630239), Humanities and Social Sciences Annual Project of Shenzhen (No. SZ2022C020).

References

1. Committee of the National People's Congress of China, Law of the People's Republic of China on Vocational Education (2022). http://www.npc.gov.cn/c2/c30834/202204/t20220420_317575.html. (in Chinese)
2. General Office of the CPC Central Committee, General Office of the State Council of China. Opinions on Deepening the Reform of Modern Vocational Education System Construction. (2022). https://www.gov.cn/zhengce/2022-12/21/content_5732986.htm. (in Chinese)
3. Ji'an, D.: Constructing the higher vocational education with practice teaching system as the core. J. Higher Educ. **2004**(04), 48–52. (in Chinese)
4. Xuan, Z., Tang, H.V.: Industry-education integration policies in china's vocational education: a bibliometric analysis of current status and development trends. Int. J. Soc. Anthropologies Sci. Rev. **2025**(03), 309–322. (in Chinese)
5. Arinaitwe, D.: Practices and strategies for enhancing learning through collaboration between vocational teacher training institutions and workplaces. Empirical Res. Voc. Ed. Train. **2021**(13), 1–22
6. Wright, M., Clarysse, B., Lockett, A., Knockaert, M.: Mid-range universities' linkages with industry: Knowledge types and the role of intermediaries. Res. Policy **2008**(8), 1205–1223
7. Dan, L.: Research on the construction of "Double Qualified Teacher" faculty team under the background of integration of production and education. Forward **2018**(05), 39–45. (in Chinese)
8. Yangqiu, Z., Lin'e, Z., Guanghong, J.: Industry-education community: connotative value, problem dilemma and path optimization. Vocat. Tech. Educ. **40**(35), 6–9 (2019). (in Chinese)
9. Yiquan, F., Yunbi, H., Liying, G.: A new exploration on the integration of industry and education in china's vocational universities based on the destiny community. J. Vocat. Educ. **01**, 128–132 (2020). (in Chinese)
10. Knudsen, H.: Higher education in a sustainable society. Springer International Publishing, pp. 147–175 (2015)

11. Yanfeng, Z., Zuocheng, H., Wen, Y., Lingquan, Z.: Exploration and practice of collaborative education model based on industrial college. Chinese Vocat. Tech. Educ. **2020**(20), 58–63. (in Chinese)
12. Yuxiang, Z.: Construction of double spiral talent training model in vocational colleges under the background of industry education integration. J. Vocat. Educ. **37**(04), 140–146 (2021). (in Chinese)
13. Zhi, W.: Thoughts on building a collaborative education community between government, enterprises, and schools in higher vocational education. Educ. Vocat. **10**, 49–52 (2018). (in Chinese)
14. Huashan, Z.: The construction of a community for the integration of industry and education in vocational education in the new era. Educ. Vocat. **05**, 5–12 (2020). (in Chinese)
15. Xue, P.: Learning community in English course: connotation, elements and construction. Educ. Res. Exp. **03**, 48–53 (2020). (in Chinese)
16. Chen Zhijie, X., Lan, L.Y., Trends, V.: Practical problems and direction choices of the construction of industry-education integrated enterprise. Educ. Vocat. **23**, 12–19 (2021). (in Chinese)
17. Enmao, Q.: Exploring the construction plan for a smart city management technology professional training lab. Telecom World **05**, 91–93 (2025). (in Chinese)
18. Cai Qingqing, F., Bin, W.J., et al.: Exploration of practical teaching in vocational information-related majors based on VR/AR. Comput. Educ. **08**, 192–196 (2024). (in Chinese)

Author Index

B
Baoqi, Wang 73

H
He, Xiaorong 1
Huang, Gaowu 45

J
Jia, Baolei 45
Jiang, Hui 81
Jisheng, Zhang 73

L
Li, Weifang 34
Liang, Changhu 1
Lin, Xiaotao 34
Liu, Dashan 81
Liu, Feifei 45

Q
Qian, Chungen 34

S
Shi, Bing 1
Shi, Mingfeng 1, 45
Shui, Jie 45
Srivastava, Aadya 15

W
Wang, Gang 34
Wang, Mengjiao 81

X
Xiang, Xufu 34
Xiangbo, Zhu 91

Y
Yang, Chenming 55
Yang, Jun 1
Yanyan, Wen 73
Yao, Lijuan 1
Ye, Kejiang 55

Z
Zhao, Yuke 1, 45

GPSR Compliance
The European Union's (EU) General Product Safety Regulation (GPSR) is a set of rules that requires consumer products to be safe and our obligations to ensure this.

If you have any concerns about our products, you can contact us on

ProductSafety@springernature.com

In case Publisher is established outside the EU, the EU authorized representative is:

Springer Nature Customer Service Center GmbH
Europaplatz 3
69115 Heidelberg, Germany

www.ingramcontent.com/pod-product-compliance
Lightning Source LLC
Chambersburg PA
CBHW071933061025
33644CB00027B/1573